FREE AUDIOBOOK ACCESS

Scan the QR code at the end of this book
to listen to a free audio recording of this book,
narrated by the author.

THE SPIRAL STAIRCASE

A MANIFESTO FOR CREATORS, REBELS, AND FOUNDERS
WHO WANT TO BUILD BRANDS AND LIVE A BOLD LIFE

THE SPIRAL
STAIRCASE

WHY I STEPPED OFF A ROCKET SHIP TO BUILD A CATHEDRAL

DAVID THURSTON

THURSTON
PRODUCTIONS

Thurston Productions
thurstonproductions.com

Cover design by Kristin Olivieri
olivieriandco.com

For Alexis
The artist.
The alchemist.
The one who climbs beside me.

And for Ted, Tev, Stevie, David
This is your legacy too.

TABLE OF CONTENTS

Prologue   xi

ACT I – The Climb

1   The Spiral Staircase   1
2   Outgunned in Long Beach   11
3   Folding Towels, Plotting Revenge   17
4   Blueprints and Butterflies   21
5   The Kung Pao Revolution   31
6   Butterfly Circus   39

ACT II – The Rocket Ship

7   Building the Riot   51
8   Hyperdrive   61
9   The Family Farm   69
10   The Flip Flop Summit   79
11   The Wires   91
12   Paris, Motherfucker   95
13   The Honeymoon   99
14   The High Life   101
15   The Slow Creep   103

16	Storm Clouds	107
17	When the Climb Stops	113
18	Signing Off	119
19	The Drop	125
20	The Calm Between the Storms	127

ACT III – The Cathedral

21	Burying the Past	139
22	Building Something Different	147
23	The Manifesto	151
24	Laying the First Stone	157
25	Danger Fest	165
26	The Malibu Pivot	173
27	The Power of Many	183
28	Catching Fire	189
29	The Nomadic CEO	193
30	The Higher Step	197
31	The Grind Behind the Glamour	201
32	Unifying the Industry	215
33	The Next Wave	211
34	The Myth of Arrival	219
35	The Spiral Continues	221

| Epilogue | 225 |
| Notes from the Climb | 231 |

PROLOGUE

It was a rainy night in Helsinki when everything changed.

Just a few hours earlier, my partner Alexis and I had lit up a packed nightclub... a sold-out show for hairstylists. We had taken the same stage show across Europe, from Madrid to Moscow, to promote the hair color brand we started called Pulp Riot.

Our shows weren't some boring corporate seminars. They were more like rock concerts. Chaos in motion.

Tattooed stylists slicing hair to a Nine Inch Nails track like it was performance art. Music so loud, you could feel it thumping in your chest. Models strutting the stage with neon hair. A wall-sized screen behind us flashing riotous visuals.

And me? I was the on-stage conductor of this creative mayhem.

After the show we stuck around for selfies. Did interviews with the press. Sunk into a shadowy booth. Laughed over cocktails with our traveling stylist team.

We were scheduled to do a show the next night in Sweden, but back at the hotel, with the adrenaline fading, I changed our plans.

Alexis would fly on to Sweden with the team.
But I was going home.
To Los Angeles.
Alone.

You see, five months earlier, a major company made an offer to buy Pulp Riot. We'd said yes, but the deal wasn't final. They first had to complete an exhaustive due diligence process.

We gave them everything:
Our financials, contracts, formulations.
Our secret sauce.
All of it.

And at any moment they could walk away. Some days it felt real. Other days, like a setup. We couldn't talk about it, not to our team, not to our friends, not even family.

There's a particular kind of madness that comes from knowing someone has offered you tens of millions of dollars and can take it away at a moment's notice.

But that night in Helsinki, we finally got the call. Due diligence was complete. The acquiring company was ready to sign. So, I cancelled my flight to Sweden and booked one to LA instead.

As I packed my suitcase, I couldn't stop thinking about how fast it all had happened. Just twenty-three months earlier, we launched Pulp Riot from our apartment in Los Angeles.

No sales reps.
No distributors.
No office.
Just one employee.

Three days before launch, Alexis and I created a make-shift assembly line in our apartment with our young daughters. We packed 500 pre-launch promo boxes, each containing five of our products. Pink, purple, blue, red, and teal hair dye. Sleek black box with magnetic closures. Every detail precise.

We wanted stylists to feel special.
Chosen.
And they did.

Within days, the beauty industry was buzzing.
Stylists posted unboxings.
Rainbow hair lit up Instagram.

Captions read: "Best product I've ever used."
And they meant it.

On launch day, I posted a photo of a model that Alexis had colored with pastel dyes. Sea Glass melted into Lilac melted into Lemon.

I wrote a simple caption:

"3...2...1," followed by the rocket ship emoji.
Everything's about to change."

I didn't know how right I was.

Because within seventy-two hours, we had orders from all fifty states and every Canadian province. Stylists even posted screenshots of their order confirmations. Proof they were in early. That they got in before the floodgates opened. And that they were cool enough to recognize it.

Three months later, over 3,000 salons were ordering our color.

The rocket ship had cleared the atmosphere.

Back in Helsinki, just before bed, I got another email. The deal was in jeopardy. A minority investor, who owned less than 1% of the company, was threatening to block the entire thing over a grudge with another investor.

You've got to be fucking kidding me.

I flew back to LA anyway, hoping proximity would help me feel some control. I felt a need to be on our home turf, close to our team, on the same time zone as our lawyers.

Thirty minutes after takeoff, I felt a cold sore forming... the kind triggered by stress.

I landed at Heathrow.

Checked email.

Nothing.

Texted my dermatologist to have antivirals ready.

Finally arrived in LA.

Grabbed a coffee.

Popped a few cold sore meds.

And made phone calls to both sides, like a U.N. diplomat, until there was finally a compromise.

At 11:30 AM, our banker said the acquirer wanted a call. No promises. Just a call.

At noon, we all dialed in.

I was in LA.

Alexis in Sweden.

And they called in from New York.

Lawyers.

Bankers.

Everyone assembled.

Silence.

Then a voice asked,
"David Thurston, do you release?"

Release? What a strange way to put it. I paused for a beat, wondering if I should clarify what they meant, but didn't want to slow things down.

"Yes. I release."

Muffled whispers in the background.

Then the voice said, "Congratulations, gentlemen."

And that was it.

Just 23 months after launching our brand with an Instagram post, we sold Pulp Riot to L'Oréal, the biggest beauty company in the world.

So, what did I do next? Blast *We Are the Champions* and spray champagne on the ceiling?

Nope.

I walked down Ventura Boulevard in a daze.
The scorching sun beating down on me.
Stepped into a Jersey Mike's.
Ordered a turkey sandwich.
No cheese.
No onions.

Sat alone.
Opened my JP Morgan app.
The first payment had already hit.

I blinked twice.
Nearly one hundred million dollars.

Holy shit.

Eight years earlier, I was 39 years old, making only $24,000 a year managing a friend's hair salon, feeling like a total failure. And now I was holding a turkey sandwich in one hand, and a fortune in the other.

I thought the climb was over.
But it wasn't.
Not even close.

This book isn't just about selling Pulp Riot. It's about everything I learned before, during, and after, and how you can use those lessons to build something that matters.

It's for anyone who knows they're meant for more but isn't sure how to start.

It's for the rebels stuck in corporate jobs.
The founders who feel like frauds.
And the artists who've lost their spark.

It's for the ones who keep climbing.
Even when they can't see what's at the top.

ACT I
THE CLIMB

1
THE SPIRAL STAIRCASE

We all get sold a lie:
Go to school.
Get good grades.
Land the job.
Work hard.
Rise through the ranks.
And eventually, you'll "make it."

They call it "the pathway to success," like it's some yellow brick road you stroll down until you arrive at the promised land.

But here's the truth:
Success isn't a path.
It's a climb.
A relentless, terrifying, beautiful climb.

And for those brave or foolish enough to try, the climb doesn't go straight up. It winds. It twists. It hides the destination from view.

The climb is like a spiral staircase. You can only see one or two steps up, but you can't exactly see where it's going.

Now, there are a couple of simple but important rules to the spiral staircase:

Rule 1 - Every time you take a step up, it's uncomfortable. Always. Because you're stepping outside your comfort zone into a new world.

Rule 2 - The discomfort is temporary. It fades. It may last a couple of weeks. Maybe a few months. But soon, that scary new step becomes your new comfort zone.

So why do so many people stay unfulfilled, or even worse, in shitty jobs or toxic relationships for 10, 15, even 20 years? Why do they vent to their friends, complain on group chats, whisper to their therapist that they're unfulfilled, and still never make a move and take a step up?

Fear.

Because they don't want to feel uncomfortable for even a second. They'd rather spend decades of quiet misery than endure two months of discomfort.

And the real tragedy isn't the wasted time.
It's all the magic they miss out on.
The people they could have met.
The places they could have gone.
The experiences, the joy, the moments of awe.

The impact they could have made on others, maybe even the world.

But here's the good news: once you learn the second rule, that the discomfort fades, everything changes.

It was the early 2000s and I was living in San Francisco, working at an international management consulting firm.

Crisp suit.
Office with a view.
Decent paycheck.
Climbing the corporate ladder.

But every day, I felt it creeping in, that quiet dread that whispers, *This isn't your life. It should be bigger than this.*

I'd go home for the holidays and tell stories about projects and promotions, because that's what success looked like, right?

My parents were proud. Others thought I was on the pathway to success. But I felt like an actor in someone else's movie.

Inside I had a wish list. Not a written one. The kind that lives in your chest.

Creative freedom.
Autonomy. Adventure. Art.
Leadership.
Living boldly.
To make a fucking dent in the universe.

One night, I asked myself a big question: will what I'm doing right now get me the things on my wish list?

I looked at my boss's life.
Then I looked in the mirror.
The answer was obvious.
I had climbed a ladder leaned against the wrong wall.

I had given my all for years, but lately I was unfulfilled. Stuck on a step for far too long. My heart had already left the building. And eventually, so did I. For good.

The spiral staircase is the journey, and it isn't random. There's a hidden engine that powers it. I call it the Commitment Cycle. It's the engine behind every bold life I've ever admired. Each time you take a step up the staircase, you activate the cycle.

Here's how it works:

1 - Commit – You take the step up.

2 - Learn – You're now on a new step, and now you're forced to figure things out. This is the part of the climb where people feel the discomfort, because learning can be uncomfortable.

3 - Grow – You develop new capabilities. You develop more skills and become more powerful. And the second rule of the spiral staircase kicks in... the discomfort starts to fade away.

4 - Confidence – Becoming more capable leads to confidence. The new step has become your new comfort zone.

5 - Repeat – Confidence gives you the courage to commit to taking another step up.

And around and around you go, like gears clicking forward. Commit. Learn. Grow. Level up. And if you keep climbing upward, you can design an extraordinary life.

But the cycle doesn't start until you do the hard part... until you commit.

It doesn't start with learning.
It starts with a leap

This cycle is the secret to designing an amazing life, and it's what saved me from a life that looked impressive on the outside but felt like a slow death on the inside.

Most people wait for everything to be perfect before they take that step. But if you're waiting for perfect conditions, you're going to be waiting a very long time.

I've found that when you commit fully, even if its messy, circumstances start to align, people appear, and opportunities suddenly reveal themselves.

Some people call it manifesting. Some call it the law of attraction. Personally, I think most of that language is kind of bullshit. But I believe in this: when you go all in, the world reacts.

That's what happened to me.

I committed, and a chapter of my life came to an end. No safety net. No clear direction.

This led to - At a dinner party, my mom told her friends I'd left my job and was thinking of doing something more entrepreneurial. It probably sounded like I wanted to join a cult.

And this led to - I got a call from Ted, an old family friend, former youth group mentor, and serial entrepreneur. He was at that dinner party.

I wouldn't have received that call if I didn't close that chapter. I committed, and the world reacted.

Ted had seen me lead when I was a kid. When I was eleven, he asked what I wanted to be when I grew up. I didn't say firefighter or pro athlete. I said entrepreneur. He never forgot that.

Ted wanted to start a hair product company in LA. He was looking for a partner. He thought I had the spark to help it happen.

It was outside my comfort zone.

I didn't know anything about the beauty industry.

I didn't know anything about building a company.

Fear kicked in.

And so I said no.

A week later, an envelope showed up. Inside: a copy of the book *Rich Dad Poor Dad* by Robert Kiyosaki. And a sticky note from Ted that read:

"It's better to own the corporate ladder than spend your life trying to climb it."

I sat on my Twin Peaks balcony, reading the book over the San Francisco skyline. One line hit me like a lightning bolt:

"You'll live your life playing it safe, doing the right things, saving yourself for some event that never happens. Then you die a boring old man."

I couldn't unread it.

I packed up my shit and moved to LA.
Not with a blueprint.
With a decision.

I told an old colleague what I was doing. He smirked and said, "Good luck becoming a hair tycoon."

The word tycoon hung in the air, exaggerated on purpose, dipped in sarcasm. He said it like I was delusional, like I was chasing a fantasy.

Maybe he didn't believe I could do it.
Or maybe he did and that scared him.

Most likely? He just didn't have the balls to climb the spiral staircase. He'd rather stay on the same step, clocking in, collecting paychecks. Keeping things safe.

Meanwhile, I had taken the step.
I committed.
I was in motion.
And the Commitment Cycle took over.

I learned. Developed new capabilities. Which in turn grew my confidence. So, when the next step revealed itself, I was ready to take it.

That moment when I walked away from comfort and climbed into chaos was the beginning of everything. Every success I've had since traces back to that decision.

It's the same decision you'll face, over and over again.

If you want a bold life, this is the deal:
You will be scared.

You will not be ready.

You will not have a plan.

You will take the step anyway.

Because the spiral staircase never shows you the top. But if you keep climbing, one step at a time, it will take you somewhere extraordinary.

This book isn't about one brand or one industry. Or one version of success. It's about committing to live a life that matters, no matter the cost.

It's about designing a life you actually want to live. It's about choosing to climb the spiral staircase.

So, take a breath. The next step on your spiral staircase is right in front of you. Climb.

2
OUTGUNNED IN LONG BEACH

Ted was in his fifties.

His resemblance to Clint Eastwood was uncanny. He looked like the actor circa 1988 in the movie *The Dead Pool*. Same jawline, same squint, same larger-than-life presence.

He was one of a kind. Lived in a Southern California suburban neighborhood where the uniform was flip-flops and cargo shorts. But Ted wore cowboy boots. No irony.

He had money. But he drove an old red Suburban that looked like it had survived the apocalypse. He called it Big Red, like it was a war horse. Somehow, he made it cool.

Ted was also a storyteller.
He had wins.
Big ones.

Among other successful ventures, he'd built the second-largest salon company in the world. And then? He got ousted by his board of directors. Cold. No thank you, no ceremony. Just a quiet, but brutal exile.

By the time we linked forces, he'd licked his wounds.
The fire was burning again.

He didn't just want to win.
He wanted revenge.

And that's how Level6, our new venture was born.

Ted didn't bankroll our venture.
He gave me something more valuable: permission.
A seat at the table.
A shot.

He taught me how to raise money. How to build a proto-type before scaling. How to protect ownership with your life, a lesson he learned the hard way, and one that's tat-tooed on my soul to this day.

But everything else?
That was on me.

I was the company.
Sales. Marketing. Education. Product. Operations.
All of it.

I drove from city to city, walking into salons uninvited. Dropped off samples. Gave impromptu presentations. Hoped, begged for someone to care.

I was obsessed.
Not because I had to be.
Because I felt alive.

Spent weekends in salons, just observing. Studying. What makes a salon feel magnetic? How do the best stylists move around behind the chair?

I was learning everything. Except how to really win.

Because we had a problem.

Eight years in, and nobody really gave a shit.

No real traction.

No buzz.

Very little spark.

Just rejection, one salon at a time.

There was no Instagram at the time.

No viral videos.

No algorithm to hack.

Just cold calls, magazine ads, and blind hope.

And still, nothing.

So, we made one last move.

A Hail Mary.

Our cash was drying up. We desperately needed awareness. So, we reserved a booth at the Long Beach hair show. A beauty industry trade show in a convention center. Ten thousand stylists would attend.

But calling it a "booth" is generous.

Picture this:

A ten-by-ten-foot square of carpet.

A table.

Bottles of shampoo lined up like soldiers.

Two folding chairs.

A stack of brochures.

A banner we printed at Kinko's.

I invited my friend Alexis to join me. She was also my hairstylist. But she wasn't just anyone behind the chair. Clients didn't visit her for the hair color. They were there for her.

She was electric.
Thin. Sharp. Edgy and elegant at the same time.
Long blonde hair. Lots of it. All California sun.
Effortlessly beautiful. No ego.

She had that thing you couldn't fake... presence.

And that's why I figured she would be the perfect person to have in my fox hole. Plus, I thought she could lend some credibility and cover the gaps in my knowledge.

The convention doors opened up.
Stylists came pouring in.
We stood there.
Ready to spring into action.
Smiling. Waving. Waiting.

But all weekend long we watched the crowds ignore us. Walk right past us. Beelining for the giant booths: the ones built by the goliath-sized companies. L'Oréal. Wella. Aveda. Paul Mitchell.

They had massive stages. Lighting that hung from scaffolding. Music pumping. Famous stylists parading around on stage with professional agency models. Crowds of stylists gathering all around.

From where we sat, their booths looked like huge casinos on the Vegas Strip.

And us?

We looked like a lemonade stand in the parking lot.

They were Goliath. And we were David, without a sling-shot or a cunning plan.

No one cared.
No one stopped.
Couldn't catch an eye, or a flash of a smile.

It broke me.

A few weeks later, Level6 flatlined. It was brutal. I was devastated. I had poured everything into it. And when it died, it felt like I did too, at least a part of me.

I questioned everything, my talent, my instincts, even my worth. I'd risked something big. And I lost.

But was it a failure?
Depends how you measure.

I learned how to manufacture hair products.
How to design packaging.
How to design brochures.
How to do my own damn bookkeeping.
How to take rejection on the chin and keep showing up.

But most of all?
I learned something that changed me forever:
You can't beat Goliath by playing his game.
You have to build something he can't.
And you can't do it alone.

Yes, failing sucked. Big time.
It was humiliating.

But the brand failed.
I didn't.

That weekend in Long Beach? That wasn't the end. Turns out, that was the first real step on the spiral staircase. I just didn't know I was climbing yet.

At the time it didn't feel like growth.
It certainly didn't feel like a climb.
In fact, it felt like falling down an elevator shaft.

But now? Now I know. That was the weekend everything quietly began. It wasn't a booth. It was a battlefield. Even though I lost, I came out with something major: a reason to fight.

And Alexis? She didn't know it yet. But her story was about to get all tangled up with mine.

And you?
Maybe you're standing at your own booth right now.
Maybe you're waving at a crowd that won't stop.
Maybe it feels like no one sees you.
Like you're outmatched.
Like you missed your shot.

But maybe, just maybe, this is your booth moment.
Your first real step.

3
FOLDING TOWELS, PLOTTING REVENGE

Level6 was dead.

And with it, my confidence.

Eight years. Gone.

No money. No offers. No roadmap.

It was 2008, during the middle of the Great Recession. No one was hiring. Especially a failed entrepreneur with a resume that wouldn't make any sense to a corporate recruiter.

All I had were lessons that I hadn't yet figured out how to turn into wins. So, I did the thing I swore I'd never do again. I took a job.

Ted threw me a life raft. And some keys. Offered me a position managing a struggling salon he recently opened called David Douglas.

The pay?

Just $24,000 a year.

From a promising career in management consulting to folding towels. From raising capital to answering phones. From a dream of building an empire to an underpaid salon manager.

It wasn't just humbling.
It was humiliating.

But here's the thing about hitting bottom: if you're paying attention, you can start to rebuild from the inside out.

After a couple of weeks of feeling sorry for myself, I flipped the narrative. This wasn't a demotion. And this wasn't a job either. It was a paid internship.

An undercover mission inside the very culture I once tried to infiltrate. An opportunity to get full access to the inner workings of salons and stylists. If I was going to disrupt the industry, I had to live inside it first.

Sometimes, in order to climb upward, it might feel like you're taking a step back, but if you zoom out, you'll realize that it's actually an important step needed to form the new connections, gain the knowledge, and develop the skills needed to leap upward.

So, I committed.
Again.
Both feet in.

I studied everything.
How stylists worked.
What made them tick.
Why they left.
Why they stayed.

I watched. I listened. I learned how to earn trust and how to build culture... not from above, but beside them.

I learned how to speak their language. Stylists don't care how you think about something. They care how you feel about something. There's a difference.

I learned that if you want to inspire them, you aim for the heart, not the head.

Slowly, the place came back to life.
Stylists started showing up with more purpose.
New talent came knocking.
The salon had a heartbeat again.

And so did I.

I didn't just manage the salon.
I transformed it.
And in the process, it transformed me.

I discovered something I never expected:
I loved being inside a salon.
Not visiting.
Not consulting.
Living inside it.

I had committed.
I had learned.
I had grown and developed new capabilities.
I turned out to be a damn good salon manager.
And I learned that I loved it.

And with those new capabilities, I grew, and my confidence came back. Not all at once. Not in some big dramatic scene. But slowly. Quietly. Folded towel by folded towel.

And then, one day a new step appeared. I didn't force it. I didn't chase it. It revealed itself the way the spiral staircase always does.

I picked up the phone.
Called Alexis.
"Hey, want to build a salon together?"

She didn't hesitate.
"Hell yeah."

And just like that, the comeback began.

4
BLUEPRINTS AND BUTTERFLIES

It was 2010. Alexis and I found a space in Los Angeles.
It was big. Maybe too big.
3,400 square feet big.

The space had been vacant for 7 years. And it was on the 2nd floor. But it had panoramic, floor-to-ceiling windows that stretched for over fifty feet, affording an epic view of the hustle and bustle of Ventura Boulevard below.

To open the salon, we took out two loans and maxed out our credit cards. We signed a five-year lease with no guarantee we could pay it off. On paper, it was a huge risk.

So why did we do it?

Because I didn't feel like I had a choice. Going back to the corporate world wasn't really an option. I'd rather fail on my own terms. And my time managing David Douglas, as chaotic as it was, gave me the most valuable thing: confidence, the kind you can't fake. The kind that makes you take the step up, even when you can't see the top of the staircase.

One big problem:
I had no idea how to build a salon.

No clue how to manage construction.
No experience with plumbing or permits.

But I didn't let that stop me. Because here's the thing: if you stick to what you know, you stay exactly where you are. You'll never climb.

So, I made a punch list. Not a master plan, just a list of everything I could think of that needed to get done, including plumbing lighting, HVAC, flooring, furniture. Then I picked one item, and I committed. That's how I've always done it. It's how you build anything that matters.

Once I commit, I just let the commitment cycle play out. I complete one item on the punch list and gain confidence to do the next.

Commit.
Learn.
Grow and develop new capabilities.
Gain confidence.
One line item at a time.

We called it Butterfly Loft.
And before I knew it, it was real.

25 styling stations.
Clean lines.
A massive color bar in the middle of the salon.
Shampoo basins with a killer view.

Stations on wheels so we could roll them out and make it an event space. A giant steel butterfly sculpture with a 6-foot wingspan hanging from the ceiling.

I took everything I learned at David Douglas salon and applied it to Butterfly Loft. With lessons learned from both mistakes and victories. For example, I learned that stylists don't just want education, they crave it. But most salon owners never provide it. I saw the gap, and I built the bridge. And a stage.

Every few weeks we would roll the styling stations off the salon floor and host education. We didn't just invite the stylists who worked at our salon. Any stylist could come.

We'd start with a cocktail party. Music up loud. The hour wasn't just hospitality. It was my chance to move through the crowd, shake hands, ask questions, make people feel seen.

I would start the education segment with a brief keynote, painting a vision of what Butterfly Loft could become. By the end of the night, at least one stylist would grab my arm on their way out and ask the magic question: "Do you have any stations available to rent?"

I also used creative pricing when it came to station rent. I could spot talented artists on the rise, people I knew would succeed if someone just gave them a shot. They couldn't yet afford big-salon rates, so I invested in them and played the long game, offering them terms that let them grow while locking in their loyalty. We would help them succeed, trusting that the investment would pay off for us both.

That's how we filled our chairs. And it worked. Almost overnight. Profitable in just thirty days. Every station rented in sixty.

And here's the thing. I wasn't working *in* the business; I was working *on* it. I was looking for the cracks in the industry, the blind spots in our competitors, the moves others couldn't see coming.

Most of the neighboring salon owners were too busy cutting hair or working behind the reception desk to notice the revolution brewing down the street. But I had my head up, my eyes open, and a room full of stylists learning that Butterfly Loft wasn't just a salon. It was the center of something they wanted to belong to.

For the first time in a long time, I felt like a success. And it was glorious. Not just because the money was good, but because the whole thing actually worked.

After building Butterfly Loft, I had developed new capabilities, which made me more confident in managing construction. So, when the space next door opened up a year later, we expanded. Added 8 more stations.

Another step up the spiral staircase.
We weren't just surviving, we were scaling.

And somewhere in the middle of all that, something else started to stir. People assumed Alexis and I were already a couple. We weren't. Not yet. We were partners. Co-conspirators. Sharpening each other's thinking.

But the long nights added up.

The laughter.

The shared ambition, and shared wavelength.

The spark.

When you spend every day solving problems together, when you trust someone with your ideas, your instincts, your ambition, sometimes that foundation turns into something more.

It happened gradually.

Then all at once.

Just two people who had built something together and realized they were building more than a business.

A year later, we were married. Inside the salon, under the giant steel butterfly sculpture. From that point on, we climbed together.

And then... then came the gut punch.

It was Saturday morning. I was curating the playlist. Downtempo poolside vibes.

One of our stylists walked in.

She said she loved working at Butterfly Loft.

She said she loved working with me.

And then she said she was leaving.

Today.

Before I could process the hurt, another stylist came in and delivered the same message. Then another, and then another.

By the end of the day, nine stylists had quit.

You see, they were going to work for a giant national chain of salon suites that had just opened up down the street. Salon suites were a relatively new model: consisting of small private studios that stylists could rent, decorate, and call their own.

Their pitch was strong.
No bosses.
No co-workers.
Play your own music.
Freedom.

The allure was so strong that it pulled nine stylists from my salon in one day.

I was gutted. Blindsided.
Felt betrayed.
Experienced physical symptoms of sickness.

Feelings of betrayal turned to feelings of terrifying concern. Was the early success of Butterfly Loft just a fluke? Was I going to fail again?

And then concern turned to anger.
I wasn't about to let another Goliath take me out.
Not again.

So, I fought back.

Called my landlord.

"Give me the space next door.

I'm going to build my own salon suites."

I learned a painful lesson with the death of Level6. If you're going to compete with Goliath, you have to offer something they can't.

After a few hours of brainstorming with Alexis, I grabbed a blank piece of paper and scribbled down three things. Not just strategies, but belief systems.

1. Build relationships.

They treated stylists like tenants, just business transactions. So, we decided we'd treat them like artists. And we'd build strong relationships with them.

2. Build the W hotel for stylists.

They designed their salon suites with shitty materials and terrible esthetics. They looked like a goddamn Best Western Motel. So, we were going to focus on design. Build modern and sleek salon suites, with premium materials and better tech.

3. Create a community.

We had a home field advantage. The corporate salon suites were isolating. Their stylists came to work, unlocked their suite, worked, locked back up and left.

So, we thought of our salon suites like Brooklyn. And Butterfly Loft salon as Manhattan. The stylists in our salon suites could simply walk over to Butterfly Loft. Collaborations. Comradery. Connection. Go to our classes. Attend our parties. And then they could go back to their salon suites and run their own show. The best of both worlds.

We got the word out. And it hit. Almost every salon suite sold out before we finished construction.

I had now completed 3 construction projects. I wasn't just building my business; I was strengthening my capabilities. And with those, my confidence started to really soar.

So, I called the landlord.

"I want more space. I'm going to build something massive. More salon suites. Double the size of the last project."

It was a bold move. I could've stopped after surviving the hit from Goliath. But I didn't just defend my ground, I went on the offense. Because now I had the skills. I had the vision. And I had the momentum to match.

And holy shit. It worked. The new salon suites pretty much sold out before the paint was dry.

It's wild to think back. When we opened Butterfly Loft, I was worried we'd never fill 3,400 square feet. A few years later, after three expansions, we were running over 10,000 square feet.

What started with twenty-five stylists had become a home for seventy.

Goliath had come for my neck again. But this time I was ready. Because I had learned the most important rule of all: you don't beat giants by playing their game. You beat them by inventing your own.

They were big.
We were fast.

They were corporate.
We were connected.

They had real estate.
But we had soul.

I wasn't just building salons anymore.
I was building something they couldn't.
Design.
Culture.
Relationships.
Community.
Creative energy that can't be franchised.

When Goliath punched, I punched back.
We didn't just survive.
We thrived.

And just when I thought we'd made it, I looked up. And saw it coming. The next tidal wave of disruption. Headed straight for us.

5
THE KUNG PAO REVOLUTION

It was 2013. From the outside, we looked unstoppable. Butterfly Loft was buzzing. Loud, alive, magnetic. But just beyond the glow of success, another storm was forming.

This one didn't come from the Goliaths.
No boardroom.
No brand.
No billion-dollar rollout.

It weighed a little less than 4 ounces.
It glowed.
And it fit in your pocket.
The iPhone.

The Butterfly Loft stylists could run credit card transactions on Square. Schedule their appointments on Outlook. And most importantly, now market themselves on Instagram.

I looked around and thought, *well, why the fuck do they need me?*

Stylists were becoming way more independent.
And most salon owners?

They responded out of fear.
Tried to keep the stylist down.
Dependent. Controlled.

And it backfired.

It drove them in waves into the arms of the salon suites, where they had total freedom.

I had a challenging puzzle to solve.
How do you lead people who don't need you?

The old models were dead. I needed to build something entirely new if I were going to keep our stylists at Butterfly Loft salon.

Not authority.
Not control.
But a platform.
A path.
A reason to rise together.

I obsessed over a single question: *How can I make stylists more successful working with me than they would be without me?*

So, I turned to Instagram, a newish social media app still finding its shape. The beauty brands didn't really know how to use it. The salons didn't really have a clue either. And only a few stylists seemed to have it figured out.

There wasn't an algorithm.
No ads. No monetization.
It was the Wild West.

I committed.
I leaned in.
Became a student.
Studied Instagram like it was my job.

I learned.
What worked.
What didn't.
What made a post land.
Angles, Lighting, Captions. Frequency. Hashtags.

I grew and developed new capabilities.
I actually became good at Instagramming.

Then, I started taking my stylists to a restaurant. Rented a private room. Ten at a time. Chinese food on me.

And while they ate Kung Pao Chicken, with confidence, I pointed to my Instagram page and said: "This is the most valuable piece of real estate that you own."

They looked skeptical.
I didn't blame them.
There was no blueprint for this.

But I told them how I saw it: "Create great content and other artists will follow for inspiration. And clients will come. Visibility is currency, and we could all be sitting on gold."

The real goal?
Definitely not dependence.
Not really independence either.

The goal was *interdependence*.
Better off together than apart.

Within weeks, I had turned 70 stylists into content creators. And I became pretty goddamn sick of Chinese food.

And then, things started to change.

Jenny posted an amazing color melt. Our salon page re-
posted it. Jenny got exposure and new followers.

Later Carrie posted a stunning blonde.
Repost.
Exposure.
More followers.

It became a rhythm.
A system.
A spotlight.
Day after day.

And then, a funny thing happened. While trying to make
them more successful, we became more successful.

Full tilt interdependence.

Our salon page exploded.
50,000 followers.
100,000 followers.
200,000 followers.

Butterfly Loft stopped being just a salon.
It became a broadcast tower.
A launchpad.

Our audience was so big, when we posted a stylist's work, it was as if they stepped out on stage at Madison Square Garden and took a bow in front of a sold-out crowd, five times over.

Butterfly Loft wasn't just marketing our salon to Los Angeles anymore. We were broadcasting to the world. Clients flew in from Brazil. France. Japan.

Stylists across the country saw us as the place to become a star. We got DMs every day asking if we had an open chair to rent. Artists ready to just pack up their shit and move out to LA, just to be a part of it all.

We helped our stylists win.
And in the process, we won too.

I committed, learned, and grew.
My confidence?
It surged.

And that's when I did something I hadn't done before.
I stepped into the light.
Put myself on camera.
To give the salon a face.
A voice.
A soul.

To say the things others were feeling, but no one was saying.

I posted why the government-mandated cosmetology school's curriculum was outdated. They weren't teaching how to use the new trendy bright vivid colors that were becoming popular, or how to build a clientele using social media.

I posted why I'd be proud if my daughters became hairstylists. Why I admired the craft, the courage, and the creativity.

I talked about dealing with haters.
How to say no.
How to raise prices.
How to succeed without selling out.
How to build salon culture.

I wrote about the stuff that doesn't make it into the textbooks. The hard-earned wisdom from working both sides of the beauty industry, as a product maker and a salon owner.

And something unexpected happened.
People listened.
My posts went viral.
Hundreds of comments.
Every single time.

People called me a damn thought leader.
Said I inspired them.
Started getting stopped at shows.
Asked for selfies.
Invited on podcasts.
Featured in beauty magazines.

When the digital tidal wave came, we didn't fight it. We grabbed surfboards and rode it.

With our phones, we were educating, inspiring, and creating trends. Things that used to be the exclusive domain of the Goliath hair product companies.

And we were doing it better.
More human.
More real.
More connected.

I was no longer just a salon owner.
I was a builder.
A connector.
A voice of the artist, coming from the underground.

6
BUTTERFLY CIRCUS

It started poolside in Costa Rica. Last day of vacation. I was reading *Never Eat Alone* by Keith Ferrazzi. One line hit like a cymbal crash in a silent room.

"The most efficient way to enlarge and tap the full potential of your circle of friends is, quite simply, to connect your circle with someone else's."

I sat up straight. Lightning strike.

I'd been using the Butterfly Loft page to educate, inspire, and create trends. And I noticed a few other artists across North America doing the same thing.

And I wondered, what if we connected our circles together? What if we joined forces, not just to grow our audiences, but build something bigger than any of us could on our own?

While I was becoming more powerful as an individual, I became obsessed with something even greater: The Power of Many.

My plan was simple. Assemble a team of top Instagram stylists. Host a live education event at Butterfly Loft. Promote it entirely through our own social media accounts.

And use our influence to sell tickets. No middlemen. No brands. Just us.

I knew who I wanted.
@larisadoll.
@passionsquared.
@lalasupdos.
@theconfessionsofahairstylist.
@jaywesleyolson.

So, I picked up the phone and called each of them. And they answered, because there really weren't a lot of brands reaching out to them. Because at this point, the brands didn't understand the power of influence. Not yet.

They were inspired by what I was posting. Grateful I reached out. And they were all in.

We weren't going to do boring education. No single educator, droning on and on for three long hours. I wanted to innovate. So, I looked to music festivals for inspiration. Each artist would get a thirty-minute set. No filler, just hits.

One would teach blonding techniques.
Another bright, vivid color techniques.
Another cutting.
Another styling.

They'd drop their knowledge for thirty minutes. Exit the stage. And work on their models while the next educator was up.

Called it Butterfly Circus. Because in a circus you also have different acts. Lion Tamer. Trapeze artist. Tightrope walker.

And me? I was like the ringleader.

While they were finishing up backstage, I'd give a 30-minute keynote to close it out. Say what others were thinking but didn't dare say, just like I was doing in my Instagram posts.

The finale? We'd bring out all the finished models, like an Instagram feed come to life.

One part education.
One part inspiration.
One part entertainment.

Stylists would learn.
But they'd feel something too.

We were audacious. Goliath brands couldn't give education away, but we decided to sell tickets for $300 a pop. Even though it was my idea, and I did the legwork, we'd split everything equally.

We each posted the same announcement on Instagram at the same time. "Tickets on sale this Friday at 7 PM."

Friday came. I refreshed the page.
Ten seconds.
Sold out.
$24,000.
Bam.

I texted the team: "We just sold out faster than a Rolling Stones concert. Want to do another show the following night?"

Jay fired a text right back:
"Fuck yeah."
Oh, it was on.

We posted again.
Sold out 2 minutes later.
Another $24,000.
Boom.

And the crazy part? Goliath never saw it happen. While I was surfing the digital tidal waves, they were sleeping through the digital revolution.

We split the $48,000 we made six ways, which meant that my Butterfly Circus team made $8,000 each for teaching just two thirty-minute segments.

We were changing the game. Taking the power from Goliath and handing it to the artists. Because we linked our circles together, each of our follower counts rocketed upward and we gained more power.

My audience started following them.
Their audiences started following me.

On the night of the show, Butterfly Loft transformed into a venue. We pushed aside styling stations. Set up chairs. Hired a guy on stilts to greet stylists at the door. Hired someone else to make cotton candy. Made it smell like a damn circus.

As the audience filed in, my Butterfly Circus team hid away in our salon suites.

I told them: "They paid $300 to be here. Show up big. Be generous. Be human. Make this night unforgettable. And no big timing. Stick around afterward for selfies."

Showtime.
We entered from behind.
The audience was seated.
We marched right to the front.
The atmosphere shifted.
The energy became electric.
Eighty phones lifted into the air.
All at once.

That was it. The spark that lit a revolution. In that moment, we weren't just stylists and salon owners anymore. We were culture shapers.

The show was a hit. Each act brought something different. They did next level hair. Shared their secrets. Told their stories with vulnerability.

After the show, no one left.
They all wanted selfies.
And we gave it to them.

You could feel it.
They weren't just entertained, they were awakened.

Fired up. Connected.
Like, they'd just seen what was possible.

I thought, if we can do this in LA, how would it go down in New York. So, I took a big swing. Rented the grand ballroom of the W Hotel on Lexington Avenue.

Invited a few new artists into the lineup, including Alexis, and a few up-and-coming influential artists: @xostylistxo.
@glamiris.
@bescene.
And a guy from the Louisiana bayou who called himself @HairGod_Zito.

Put tickets on sale.
Sold out in 7 minutes.
$80,000 for one show.

Divided it equally among the artists.
Alexis and I splitting just one share.

We kept going, like a traveling rock band.
Vegas.
Chicago.
San Francisco.
Miami.
Dallas.
Calgary.
DC.

Every show grew our influence. We weren't just throwing events. We were building community. Stylists felt seen. Inspired. Included.

Everyone wanted to be part of the Butterfly Circus team. And I was gaining a new reputation: Star Maker. Because everyone I tapped for the show became a star.

You see, it was a system. I'd link our circles to theirs. Blow them up and give them a bigger platform and exposure.

Butterfly Circus was our slingshot.
Big brands had the money.
But we had the network.

While they held committee meetings, we lit group texts on fire. While they waited for legal to approve a flyer, we sold out a show in seconds.

We moved fast.
And that was our superpower.

We went from underground to everywhere.
Magazines finally started putting us on the cover.
Brands started calling, offering deals.
Trying to buy in.
Trying to buy us.

We said no.
Butterfly Circus wasn't for sale

It wasn't a company.
It was an indie movement.

It showed what was possible when you combine social media, artist creativity, and the Power of Many.

And it showed me something else.
I had the vision.
I had the skills.
I had the network.

And as I climbed the spiral staircase, each step had given me a tool:

At Level6-
I learned how to build a company.
How to create products from scratch.

At David Douglas salon-
I learned how to speak to stylists.
How to lead, inspire, and move them.

At my salon, Butterfly Loft-
I built a brand.
I built *my* brand.
Gained confidence.
And I mastered how to really connect with artists through Instagram.

At Butterfly Circus-
I forged real connections.
Linked our circles together.
Built a community.

And now? When we worked together? We could spread a message faster and further than Goliath ever could.

One step at a time, the spiral prepared me.

Lessons learned.

Capabilities developed.

Confidence gained.

And it gave me Alexis, my ride-or-die partner-in-crime.

It was time.

Time to go after Goliath.

Time to go to war.

ACT II
THE ROCKET SHIP

7
BUILDING THE RIOT

We had the audience. The stage. The microphone.

And more than anything, we had a community of artists who were hungry for something new. Something real.

We didn't sit down one day and decide to launch a color brand. It started gradually, behind the scenes. Beneath the buzz of Butterfly Circus, between flights, after hours in the salon. Not with a business plan, or with funding.

But here's the thing:
We weren't chemists.
We were artists.
And that?
That was our edge.

We didn't have lab coats.
We had a color bar.
We had Butterfly Loft salon.
A temple of creativity.

So, after hours, when the lights were off and the doors were locked, we did what we knew best. We turned up David Bowie real loud, and mixed dyes like mad scientists. Chasing that perfect shade.

No chemical degrees on the wall, just years of working in the salon, and the raw, unfiltered energy of artists trying to create something that felt new.

We were creating vivid hair colors: those bright, unapologetic dyes that were becoming less underground every day, like pink, purple, yellow, and blue. They could be used on their own or melted one into another to make a rainbow. When we got one right, we snapped a photo. Jotted notes. Swatched it on a test strand. Then, we took it to the lab and said, "Make this real."

And they did.
Again.
And again.
And again.

Every time they sent us a new batch, we tested it on real models in the salon. Tweaked it. Sent it back.

Real salon.
Real hair.
Real pressure.
Real artists, polishing the colors into true perfection.

We wanted pigment that punched, and we got it.

Our chemists were amazed. What would take most legacy brands six months, we did in six weeks.

We needed the packaging to match the energy.
We needed it to scream, "This is different."

We were standing at the color bar, surrounded by the same tired, boring boxes and tubes everyone had seen for decades. They looked like leftovers from the Cold War.

"Why does every color line look like it was designed by an accountant?" I asked, tossing another box aside.

"Because they probably were," Alexis said, smirking.

We were going to flip the script. Each carton would be unique. Red dye in red boxes. Green dye in green boxes. Every box would look like street art, something artists would actually want to display on their color bars, not hide away in a cabinet.

Now this may not seem like groundbreaking stuff, but in a world dominated by corporate giants that thought of hair color as just some technical product, this was an innovation. It wasn't just about the color, it was also about the art.

Our tubes looked like acrylic paint. Because that's exactly what they were. Paint. For the artists.

When we designed a few prototypes, we handed them to a few Butterfly Loft stylists. The response was immediate. Their eyes lit up. Oh yeah... we had them.

Next up: the name. I couldn't decide between Pulp - The colorful dye inside the tubes reminded me of fruit juice. Or Riot - The thing we wanted to bring to the industry.

Should it be Pulp or should it be Riot?

And then it hit me. Boom.

Pulp Riot.

It was strong.
Punched you in the gut.
Made you sit up and pay attention.
It was a name you could chant.
Pulp! Riot! Pulp! Riot!

I decided to reward several artists from our Butterfly Circus team with equity. The idea was simple, but powerful: harness the Power of Many, artists and founders working side by side, to spread our message, spark early buzz, and give the brand instant momentum.

In an industry where no one could name the faces behind the product lines, I wanted to change the narrative. Imagine a brand whose owners were some of the most recognizable artists in beauty. Stylists wouldn't just buy the products; they'd feel connected to the people creating them.

But we still needed cash. It was all well and good to have product and packaging, but without money, we couldn't do shit.

We had committed without having everything already worked out. And just as it always does, the universe stepped in.

I got an email.

"You don't know me. I work behind the scenes. I like what you and your wife are doing. Let's talk."

It was signed: Tev Finger, CEO of Luxury Brand Partners.

I read the cryptic message twice.
What kind of name is Tev Finger?
Sounded like a Bond villain I thought.

A quick Google search later, and I found Tev's resume. Bumble & Bumble. Oribe. R+Co. The man was legit. Heavily involved in creating several beauty empires.

A few days later, Alexis and I were in Miami, sitting across from Tev in the sleek offices of Luxury Brand headquarters.

Tev was the kind of guy who didn't need a title. He had a presence. A quick wit. A mind that could process a thousand ideas at once. Both crazy smart and funny as hell, as if Bill Gates and Conan O'Brien had a baby.

He made the conversation feel effortless, but I knew he was sizing us up. He had us come to Miami to get to know us, and to discuss having our Butterfly Circus team at one of their events. They thought we could help fill the arena.

After some pleasantries, we pulled the switcheroo. Slid a confidentiality agreement across the table.

"Listen," I said, "I've got something to show you."

We pitched him hard with Pulp Riot's blueprint, the army of artists in our corner, and how the industry had gone faceless and soulless.

"Imagine," I said, "a brand where every stylist and salon owner can connect the faces of a brand with the logo. And those faces? Some of the biggest heroes in the stylist community."

Tev's eyes lit up.
He was all in.
Agreed to invest all of the money we needed to get going.

But then, I dropped the bomb.

"Alexis and I will be the only board members, and there will be no way to ever remove us from the board."

That killed the deal... dead in its tracks.
Silence for weeks.

But Tev hadn't built his career by giving up easily. A few weeks later, he and his team showed up in L.A., toured our salon, and slipped into the back row of a packed, high-energy Butterfly Circus show.

Saw it live.
Experienced the buzz.
The energy.
The house on fire.

We agreed to meet up again at the salon the following morning. When the Luxury Brand contingent arrived, we were in the midst of our first pre-launch Pulp Riot event.

Twenty-four of the world's top colorists. Twenty-four models. Pre-production Pulp Riot color in giant gallon containers sat on the color bar. We must have looked like the epicenter of cool.

The artists and the models had just arrived, and as a host, I was busy greeting everyone, making sure each guest felt welcome. The timing couldn't have been worse, so I told the Luxury Brand team I was swamped. Asked them to head downstairs and kill some time at the coffee shop.

An hour later they returned to a different scene: music thundering, artists painting rainbows, the whole salon alive.

Tev and I ducked into one of our spa treatment rooms. He pulled a napkin from the coffee shop out of his pocket, slid it across the table.

He said, "If we agree to the five terms on this napkin, do we have a deal?"

I scanned the words, quickly zeroed in on line five: "You and Alexis will always be the only members of the board."

I smiled, stood up and shook his hand.

We had the money.
We had the product.

We had the packaging.
We had the name.
We had the community.
Now, it was time to light the fuse.

Time to launch this rocket and see what it can do.

June 14, 2016.

We didn't have a distributor or sales rep.
We didn't spend money on advertising.
We only had one employee.

We didn't know if it was going to be just a small flicker or an inferno. We didn't want to spend all of our money on inventory. But we also didn't want to run out of products either. We needed to stay in control.

So, we created an online shop. To enter the shop, you had to input a secret code.

We sent out the first 300 codes.
The DMs flooded in.
"What's the code?"
"Can I get in?"
"Tell me the password!"

It was unintentional, but the illusion was perfect.
A velvet rope wrapped in digital code.
 A nightclub with no visible bouncer.

Everybody wanted in, because they couldn't get in.

What no one knew is that the password feature wasn't even real. You could type in anything, and it would let you in.

The secret wasn't the code.
The secret was the anticipation.

In just the first three days, orders came in from all fifty states and throughout Canada. Every week we would issue more and more codes. Thousands of orders poured in. In month three alone, we sold to over 3,000 accounts.

No sales team.
No ads.
No gimmicks.
Just a full-fledged Riot.

And Goliath?
They were asleep.
Didn't even see us coming.

8
HYPERDRIVE

Three months.

That's how long it took before Goliath came knocking.

Salon Centric. A massive distributor owned by L'Oréal.
Their stores were everywhere.
Their sales reps were everywhere.
And suddenly, they wanted us.

Salon Centric was one of two giants where most stylists shop. The other is Cosmo Prof.

I flew out to Salon Centric headquarters in St. Petersburg, Florida. Rows of cubicles, buzzing phones, people in business casual. A different world from ours, but a world that made sense. They were organized, disciplined, and built to scale.

You could feel it in the air.
They didn't know what to make of us.
We were weird.
Fast.
Loud.
Unpredictable.
Exactly what they needed.

When I got home, I sent them a letter. Not a pitch. A challenge.

"No hair color brand has ever launched with this kind of buzz. That's because we worked in reverse; we spend years building our powerful personal brands first, then we created the products. While most are trying to avoid getting crushed by the waves of change, we're riding them straight to the top. Ride with us, and you won't just benefit from profits, you'll benefit from our innovations."

It was bold. Perhaps even brash for a CEO of a three-month-old startup to tell a billion-dollar company how it is. But it showed them that we were serious enough to play on their level, and to their credit, they saw it as confidence instead of arrogance.

And it worked. Weeks later, we signed an exclusive distribution agreement with Salon Centric.

The first purchase order?
$1 million.

And then, before they even stocked the shelves, another million-dollar purchase order came in. Kaboom.

Our lab couldn't keep up. They bought a new filling machine from France. Added a second shift. Worked around the clock.

And just seven months after our first Instagram post, Pulp Riot launched in over 800 stores. And the Salon

Centric sales reps were ready to hit the streets with our product.

A launch of this magnitude is expensive. We needed more capital fast. So, I raised another $500,000 from investors. But this time, the valuation was $10 million.

We weren't selling a dream anymore.
We were selling proof.

We picked up some new investors, Doug and Stevie Theoharis, salon owners from Maryland. They believed so deeply that they went into a bank and took out a loan. Invested it in Pulp Riot.

And they didn't just write checks.
They packed up their lives.
Moved their family to LA.
Joined the team full-time.
Stevie led marketing, and Doug led education.

That's what this brand did.
It pulled people toward the fire.
It turned belief into boldness.

The riot was growing. We moved headquarters from the back patio at Butterfly Loft into Regis, a shared office space. We crammed into offices next to insurance agents and tax lawyers.

They wore suits.
We wore tattoos.
You could spot us from a mile away.

Inside our new HQ, I tried to keep the rocket ship from imploding... to bring order to the chaos. I needed to simplify. So, I scribbled our strategy on the wall:

1. Create more products
2. Grow across the world
3. Don't run out of products
4. Unify the artist community
5. Shoot giant flares into the sky

The last one? It meant to do audacious things, take bold risks, and make sure everyone was watching.

And then came Long Beach.

The trade show.

Back to the scene of the crime.

The very show where ten years earlier, back in the Level6 days, Alexis and I sat in a tiny 10-by-10-foot booth, and watched stylists walk past us like we were invisible.

This time?

We went big.

We spent $300,000 to build the biggest, most talked about booth at the show.

Overheard on the show floor...

CEO A: "Who the hell are these Pulp Riot guys?"

CEO B: "I don't know, but I heard they have more money than God."

They didn't realize that we spent almost everything we had on that booth. Because we had momentum, we were swinging for the fences. Shooting giant flares into the sky. And it worked. We were impossible to ignore.

It wasn't just a booth. It was a monument to all of the hard work. The grind. The risk taking. The manifestation of every step I climbed since Level6 flatlined. It was also a neon warning shot aimed at the heart of Goliath.

The booth had a big stage.
Stylists in combat boots.
Models in band tees.

The screen behind them spun a giant vinyl record splattered with hair color, like a Pollock painting.

We were heroes to the very stylists who ignored us ten years earlier. It was bigger and sweeter than we could have ever scripted.

We weren't going in circles.
We were spiraling upward.
That booth became our church.
And that weekend became our baptism.

We had created a land of opportunity. A platform for our devoted stylists to take to the stage and shine. "This wasn't on my bingo card," one said, shaking her head in disbelief as she stepped off our stage. Others whispered that next year, they wanted to be up there.

But when the music died down and we assembled back in our offices, reality hit hard. We were exhausted. Burned out from the pace. The team was running on fumes.

Orders were piling up, and I hadn't had a real day off in months. I wondered how long we could keep sprinting at this speed without breaking something.

When a company grows at a breakneck pace, you make tradeoffs. You invest in the parts that drive growth: marketing, sales, community, and tell yourself you'll figure out the rest later. We supported stylists. We hired content creators. We invested in education and took swings that were expensive, and risky, but they paid off. What we didn't do, at least not fast enough, was invest in infrastructure. Operations. Logistics. Finance. The behind-the-scenes engine that makes the thing actually run.

The truth is, when everything is working, you don't feel the cracks. Until suddenly, you do. Growth masks operational weaknesses, until it doesn't. And by the time you realize you need to upgrade the back end of the business, it's already too late. You're already mid-air, trying to rewire the plane while keeping it flying. We had scaled demand to a point where we couldn't ignore it anymore. And that pressure was building. Quietly. Relentlessly.

Meanwhile, our content machine was going full throttle.

After Stevie invested in Pulp Riot and moved her family to Los Angeles, she quickly went about the business of building out a marketing team. Videographers. Designers. Creatives crammed into a tiny office like a war room.

Let me tell you about Stevie. She didn't come from the corporate world. She basically grew up in her dad's hair salon. Started by sweeping floors. Eventually ran the place.

She didn't have experience working in a corporate setting, and it showed.

Long jet-black hair.
Tight pants.
Cropped tops.
A wardrobe that didn't ask permission.
Decidedly not business casual.

She walked through our building full of men in suits like she owned the place.

They'd do double-takes.
Whisper.
Stare.
She didn't notice.
Or maybe she didn't care.

But Stevie... she just *got it*. Saw things the way I did. She brought organization to chaos. Smart. Practical. Made sure the trains ran on time.

Plucked her from the salon and made her head of marketing for Pulp Riot. Saw something in her that she didn't see in herself. Because of that she was grateful. And loyal. The fiercest of allies.

Every morning, she sat in my office. We'd riff. Brainstorm. She took notes on her iPad like she was recording scripture. By afternoon, the content was shot. By evening, it was posted.

Alexis built a product development team. Her office was another creative bunker. Swatches everywhere. Walls covered in launch calendars and formulations.

Her experience as a stylist made her the perfect product creator. Her fingers were always stained with little streaks of magenta or turquoise that no soap could scrub off. A mark of creation she wore like jewelry.

I floated between the teams.
Marketing.
Product.
Sales.
Strategy.

Every day was chaos.
And every day was magic.
Pulp Riot wasn't a brand anymore.
It was a full-blown movement.

And the industry giants? They could no longer miss the huge flares we were shooting into the sky.

9
THE FAMILY FARM

One year after we launched, and just five months since we launched with Salon Centric, we rolled into the biggest hair show in North America, Premiere Orlando. When we arrived, our big ass tradeshow booth was already standing in the center of the convention center, like a shining monolith in a sea of beige.

Just twelve months earlier, I was hunched over my phone in our small apartment, uploading a single Instagram post.

"Everything's about to change," the caption read. At the time, it felt like hope. But now it was starting to feel like a prophecy.

We had just got off an enormous stage. A legion of passionate artists filing out of the amphitheater. My head already switching gears from Orlando to Australia. Soon I would be headed there to launch Pulp Riot "down under."

My phone buzzed.
A text from the President of Salon Centric.
"David Greenberg wants to meet you.
He's the top dog at L'Oréal.
Keep it confidential.
Don't tell anyone."

It was surreal. I stared at the screen, and it didn't make sense. It felt like being summoned by the godfather. Or the man behind the curtain.

I showed up the next morning full of nervous curiosity. Walked through the hotel lobby, and there was David Greenberg.

Tall. Trim. Confident. A neatly groomed mustache. Dressed in the kind of effortless polish that says: *I play at a higher level.* He had a sideways grin like he already knew something I didn't.

We sat in the back of the restaurant, right next to the editor of Modern Salon and the editor of American Salon, two of the biggest professional beauty magazines in the world. So much for being confidential.

He made small talk.
Sipped his coffee.
Then his eyes lit up.

"I've been following the Pulp Riot journey closely. Your brand gives me goosebumps. I haven't felt that from a beauty brand in a long time. I think Pulp Riot would fit quite nicely in the L'Oréal portfolio."

Wait. What?

A year earlier we were listening to David Bowie, swatching out colors in our salon. And now the biggest beauty company in the world was thinking about buying our punk rock band?

As the next few months rolled by, David and I would check in here and there. He was monitoring our progress.

The good news?
We were growing like hell.
Sales were exploding.
Demand was high.

However, it was right after my meeting with David that some serious cracks started to surface, because the kind of success we were experiencing often comes with a hidden trap, one that can get really messy when you ignore building out the infrastructure to support an insane level of growth.

You see, we had to keep inventory high to avoid out-of-stocks. As salon owners, we knew that if you run out of products, you break the trust. Stylists switch. You lose them for good.

So, we made a choice.
A bet, really.
Prioritized inventory over cash.
Figured we'd sell through it soon enough.

But here's the catch: if you choose wrong, it can kill you. And then, it happened.

Salon Centric stopped ordering. No warning. Just a full stop. Unbeknownst to us, they had too much inventory. Without warehouse visibility, we were flying blind. All we saw was the silence. And because we prioritized growing our marketing and sales departments, we didn't have the expertise to help guide me on important operations-related decisions that I was underqualified to make on my own.

And now? We were in trouble. We had mountains of product and almost no cash. We were bleeding money. Marketing was expensive. Payroll loomed. And the runway was shrinking fast.

It was crazy. On one hand, I was having conversations with L'Oréal about selling the company. On the other hand, I was trying to figure out how we were going to pay next month's expenses. Almost daily, I was experiencing huge swings of emotions as I was concurrently dealing with the highs associated with opportunities and the lows that come when you're experiencing significant challenges.

Would they still want us if they knew the truth, that we were gasping for air?

We weren't in trouble long-term. In fact, I created a spreadsheet. It showed our monthly sales. Our growth rate. Proof it was just a cash hurdle. If we could somehow make it through a couple more months, we would sell through enough inventory, turn products into cash, and be okay again.

I went to a friend for a bridge loan.
Showed him the spreadsheet.
Opened our financials.

He said yes. No problem.

He passed me off to his finance guy.

Then came the stall.

Weeks passed with vague replies.

By the time our desperation peaked, he finally came back. Not with the loan we'd discussed. But with an offer to buy equity at a valuation far lower than what we believed it was worth. I had no time to be offended. The offer was far too low for me to consider. I needed to find a solution quick.

We were deep. Dangerously close to the edge. And still, I kept showing up. Kept corresponding with David Greenberg like everything was fine.

I was terrified. But I didn't flinch.

Then, just when it felt like we might go under, I got a message. Greenberg and his leadership team wanted to meet with me via Skype.

It was only seventeen months since we launched. I took the call in our conference room. That's when they made it real. A cash deal. A really big number. Plus, a potential earn-out tied to future performance.

And one more thing: They wanted me to stay on as CEO. In fact, they insisted.

It was as if, one minute I was drowning, and the next minute someone threw me a life preserver.

When I got home, Alexis was in the kitchen making us a Thai curry. We both knew I had news to share. She wanted to ask but didn't. I wanted to tell her but didn't. The news felt like it was too big to just start sharing.

I poured her a glass of Reisling and finally just blurted it out.

"They offered a little over thirty million dollars cash," I said, as I perched on the counter. Tried to say it without smiling. But couldn't.

She dropped the spoon.
"Holy fuck. That's life-changing money."

Just a year earlier, we were sitting cross-legged on the apartment floor, assembling promo boxes with our daughters, elbows deep in cardboard and hair dye. Packing tape stuck to Alexis's arm. And now, here we were, staring down eight figures.

We debated it like philosophers with too much to lose. One day, I'd argue we take it. She'd argue we wait. The next, we'd switch sides.

Dear reader, take a moment and step into my shoes.
Let's say you did the following:
Graduated college with an economics degree.
Got a solid job as a management consultant.
Left the stable job to take a big swing.
Crashed and burned. Felt like a failure.
Worked for just $24,000 a year.
But then you climbed and climbed.

Clawed your way out of the hole.

Took another swing. Another hair product line.

You were close to running out of money.

Saw potential for another huge failure on the horizon.

And then... someone offered to buy it from you. Offered more than thirty million dollars.

Be honest. Would you have taken it, or would you have walked away?

If you had told me when we started Pulp Riot, that we would one day even consider walking away from an offer of that size, I would have told you to get the fuck out.

But here we were, considering turning it down. Why? Because, we had so much runway for growth. We hadn't launched some of the more mainstream color products yet, like a permanent color line, or a gloss toner line.

Plus, we were just starting to go international. And the world is a big place, with a lot of potential customers to convert.

So, what did we do? We walked. Turned it down. And when we did, the number echoed through our apartment like a secret we couldn't shake.

And then, nothing happened.

No confetti.

No cheering.

No parade of congratulatory texts.

Just silence.

I sat on the couch in the dim light of our apartment. The hum of the fridge in the background. I stared at the ceiling, heart pounding, asking myself over and over: *Was this the moment I'd replay in my head for the rest of my life. The one where everything unraveled?*

The offer was real.
The money was real.
But so was our ambition.
So, I got to work.

I called my parents.
It was a very challenging call for me to make.
Told them about the deal we turned down.
Told them we were running out of money.
Asked for a bridge loan that I'd pay back in a few months.
It was the last resort.
Desperation.

I was concerned about borrowing from them. I felt like it would be too much weight on my shoulders. But they surprised me. Believed in what we were doing. They asked if it could be an investment instead. So, I sold some equity to them, at a fair valuation, much higher than what was offered to us a week earlier.

Now we had cash.
Now we had options.

After turning down L'Oréal's offer, I arranged a call with the president of another billion-dollar global beauty company to gauge their interest, and to see how they might value our company. On the call, I confidently justified a bold asking price. Told them our revenue would double once we released a permanent color line.

His tone shifted.
I'd struck a nerve.

He said something like, "Permanent hair color is our family farm. It pays for all of our buildings across the world. If you step onto our family farm, we will shoot you dead."

It felt almost as if he wanted me to know exactly how high the stakes were.

That lit a fire in me.
Challenge accepted.

I decided right then and there.
We would step onto the family farm.
We'd launch permanent hair color.

If we were going to play this game, we needed to play it loud.

10
THE FLIP FLOP SUMMIT

I needed to think.
To get off the grid.
Shake the sand out of my head.
Ask myself what the hell I was really doing.

So, I rented a beach house. Not just any house. A glass-walled beauty right on the sand, with waves crashing so close it felt like the ocean might crawl into bed with you at night.

It was warm for winter. Golden, glowing. A little too perfect. Like the universe was nudging us to think bigger.

The crew was small; just five of us. Alexis, Stevie, and me. Also, employee number one, Tyler. And a recent hire, a Brit named Paul. Colleagues, sure. But also, friends. Teammates. Co-conspirators.

We wore shorts and flip flops.
Ate fish tacos.
Let the sun hit our faces.

After the multi-million dollar offer, something shifted. Before that, we were just building. Focused. Hungry. Head down, eyes on the craft. We didn't talk about exits. We didn't fantasize about a finish line.

We were 18 months in; still in the thick of it. Still in love with it. But once that offer came in, everything changed. After turning it down, I couldn't un-hear the number. I couldn't un-feel the temptation.

It followed me around like a shadow.
Distracting.
Haunting.
Warping how I saw the road ahead.

We spent two days wrestling with one big question: Do we forget the offer and go back to how it was? Back to building something long-term, without thinking about a payday?

Or do we go all-in? Turn this into a sprint. Make selling the company the priority. Try to create a moment so loud and undeniable, they'd have to come back with more.

I asked the team to walk the beach alone and think.
Thirty minutes each.
No phones.
Just the sound of the waves and their own damn thoughts.

When we regrouped, there were arguments.
Passion.
Conflicting instincts.

I listened to each argument carefully.
But the truth is, I already knew.
I just needed to hear everything out loud.

I couldn't go back to how things were before.
Not really.

So, I made the call.
We'd sprint.
Hard and fast.

We'd tease a new permanent color line. Even though we hadn't made a single tube. Even though we didn't have the millions of dollars needed to create it.

My team looked confused, so I laid it out for them.

"We don't have to launch permanent color yet. We just need to make them believe it's coming. And that it's going to change everything. We have to make them believe that we'll disrupt the permanent color category, just like we did with our vivid colors."

Tyler stood up, pacing.
Rubbing his hands together.
"We've got to run as fast as we fucking can."

I agreed: full blitz.
Shoot giant red-hot flares into the sky.
Let the industry see us coming.
Hear us roar.
Give L'Oréal and others a choice.
Buy us now or pay much more later.

Twelve days later, I was in Dallas, standing on the stage at the Salon Centric National Convention, addressing close to one thousand of their sales reps and store managers.

The room was dark. Bright lights staring me in the face. I could barely see through the darkness. But there they were, L'Oréal execs standing in the back.

At the end of my presentation, I went all Steve Jobs on them: "Oh, and one more thing..."

Cue video. The most tantalizing teaser ever made. Faction8, a new permanent color line from Pulp Riot. The video was edgy, bold, haunting. It switched back and forth between a tattoo artist tattooing an arm to a stylist coloring hair, linking permanent color to the permanence of a tattoo.

"Faction8" fades in to view. "Faction" fades out, leaving just the number 8 on the screen. Then the 8 slowly turns ninety degrees to become the infinity sign. Another nod to permanence.

The final frame was a bold proclamation that splashed across the screen: "It's our turn!"

I could hear an audible gasp for two beats.
Three beats of silence.
And then it hit.
A tidal wave of applause crashed toward me.
Thunderous.
Relentless.
The kind that tells you that something shifted.

We posted the same video on Instagram the next day. The internet exploded. And I suspect L'Oréal got nervous.

Because they came back.
With more money.
A shit ton of money.

Greenberg called.
"We're increasing our offer."

My jaw hit the floor.
Close to a hundred million dollars.
Guaranteed.

Let me tell you something. When you're all of a sudden confronted with that kind of cash, your mind gets fuzzy. And you do some crazy things. Perhaps even get a little greedy.

You think to yourself, if they went from a lower number to a number much higher, it should be easy for them to go even higher still.

So, I said it: "Pulp Riot has a buy-it-now price, and you're not there yet."

He let out a deep breath.

"This is our final offer. This is not a negotiation."

He sounded really serious.
Then he hung up.
Silence.
No "we'll think about it."
Just, click.

The line went dead, but the silence in the room was deafening. I sat there frozen, the phone still warm in my hand. The air suddenly felt heavier, like gravity had turned up a notch.

Just me and the voice in my head whispering: *What the fuck did you just do?*

For the rest of my entire life, would I be telling the story of how I could have had close to a hundred million dollars? If Pulp Riot crashed and burned, would I even be able to live with myself?

Could I look my daughters in the eye each morning in our crammed Studio City apartment knowing I could have given them a different life?

And then came the counterpunch.

A few weeks later, we returned back to the Long Beach trade show. The second time for Pulp Riot.

One of our top artists who'd worked with me since the Butterfly Circus days, announced backstage that he was leaving Pulp Riot to join L'Oréal's brand called Matrix.

A punch to the gut.

They planned to make him the face of a new vivid color line they were creating in-house. A direct competitor to Pulp Riot.

It felt like a shot across the bow.
Message received.
Loud and clear.

If they could buy him, they could buy everyone.

We had the Power of Many.

They had the Power of Money.

And it looked like they weren't afraid to use it.

I stood over the kitchen island with a spreadsheet on my laptop. A cup of coffee in my hand. Alexis leaned on the counter, arms crossed, eyes scanning the numbers.

"This is how it plays out," I said.

"Scenario A.
We launch permanent color.
We go global.
We drive up our valuation.
Maybe L'Oréal comes back with a bigger offer."
I looked up at her. "It's possible."

She didn't say anything. Just kept staring.
Then I flipped the screen.

"Scenario B.
We can't raise the money.
Or Amazon enters our industry.
Or another brand leapfrogs us.
Or perhaps one of the Goliath brands crushes us before we get there.

And then?
We're not heroes anymore. We're a cautionary tale."

Silence.

She calmly said, "There's only one way to take the risk off the table. One way to make sure it doesn't all slip through our fingers."

It sunk in. Alexis and I locked eyes. We knew what we needed to do.

I called L'Oréal. Told them we were in. If I were them, I would have told me to fuck off. But they didn't, thank God. They were still interested.

But it wasn't a done deal yet. Due diligence dragged out. Four long months. Opening our vault to a company that was building their version of us. Every sales doc, every supply chain map, every strategy. All while hearing whispers about their in-house Pulp Riot killer.

Finally, they flew me to New York to meet the top brass.

New York has a way of making you feel small.
Tall buildings. Crazy traffic.
Everyone in a rush to get somewhere important.
And today, I was one of them.

Paul and I flew in the night before.
Got some sleep.
And in the morning, we met in the hotel lobby.
Didn't say a word.
We both knew what this was.
This wasn't a meeting.
This was the moment.

We took a taxi to Hudson Yards. I was in a mode I'd only ever felt a few times in my life. Still. Cold. Focused. Like an assassin in a movie. Calm. Composed. Listening to classical music in my head. Knowing exactly what needed to be done.

Hudson Yards was their turf.
Over thirty floors up.
Floor-to-ceiling windows.
Statue of Liberty in the distance.
An impressive home field advantage.

A dozen of L'Oréal's power players lined the boardroom table. Cameras linked to Paris. Suits starched to the max.

And then there was me. Tattoos. Unmistakably Californian. But I wasn't there to blend in. I was there to make them feel something.

I started seated. Calm. Measured. But within a few minutes, I was on my feet.

I showed them graphs which showed our social media engagement was higher than all of the other hair color lines. I shared stories about what our movement meant to our loyal community of artists. I showed them images of our products next to theirs and asked them which packaging they preferred.

I could see it in their eyes.
Body language shifting.
Shoulders leaning in.
They weren't just listening.
They were captivated.

At the end, I said there were five reasons Pulp Riot was a rocket ship. Each one landed harder than the last.

Then came the final and most important reason.

I paused.
Let it hang.
They leaned in.
Waiting.
Guessing.

I slowly raised my index finger into the air. Their eyes followed. Then I clicked forward, and I pointed at the screen.

"The biggest reason we're successful...
Because we're cool."

They blinked.
It wasn't what they expected.
And then, it landed.
Smiles.
Nods.

I said, "In our industry, cool is everything. It's not something you can just manufacture. Either you have it, or you don't.

And Pulp Riot?
We're not just a cool brand.
We're *the* cool brand."

Mic drop.

And that's when one of them leaned forward and told us they didn't want to "L'Oréalize" Pulp Riot, but instead, they wanted to "Riotize" L'Oréal, meaning to keep the independent spirit of Pulp Riot intact.

Afterward, as we stepped into the hallway, she grabbed my arm and whispered: "That was the best presentation I've ever witnessed."

And Paul? He turned to her and said, "When you buy Pulp Riot, you don't just get the brand. You get David. The biggest asset of all."

A month later, the phone rang.

"David, do you release?"

"I do."

The first payment was wired.

Grabbed my phone. The same one I used 23 months earlier to launch Pulp Riot with that prophetic Instagram post.

Opened my Chase banking app.

And stared at a number that didn't feel real.

11
THE WIRES

The day after our money hit, I walked back into the world I once left behind, the world of traditional business. Not my management consulting job back in San Francisco. Instead, the offices of JP Morgan.

Black t-shirt.

A list of routing numbers in my tattooed hands.

Across the desk, a young banker sat in a stiff suit. He glanced at the list, then at me. He had no idea what this moment meant.

One by one, he began wiring large sums of money to everyone who ever bet on me.

My parents were first. They stepped in when we were drowning. I watched the screen as the transfer processed. Chest tight. This was the proudest moment of my life.

Then to the individual investors, like Stevie and Doug. They borrowed money to invest in Pulp Riot. A reckless move, by most standards. But sometimes the biggest rewards go to those willing to leap without a net. They came out of this looking like Warren Fucking Buffet.

I thought back to the days of eating ramen and feeling like a total failure when my first brand crashed and burned, and I had to settle for a $24,000 a year salary. The lean years. And to when Alexis and I had to max out every credit card we had in order to get our salon off the ground.

Then I sent wires to a few key artists: Jay, Ash, and Iris. Years earlier, I'd done something no other founder in our industry was doing. I gave equity to many of the artists from my Butterfly Circus team. Not because I had to. But because I believed in shared ownership... in rewarding the people who sparked the movement.

But soon afterward, "social media influencing" became a mainstream thing. Brands started calling them. Some of the artists forfeited their equity to chase opportunities from other brands. Looking back, I can't really blame them. And they did pretty well for themselves.

But Jay, Ash, and Iris stayed loyal. They bet on the long game. Valued their equity more than chasing quick cash. And they were rewarded for doing so.

Jay used the payout to build a house.
Ash built a salon.
Iris bought property.

The banker kept looking at me like I was some kind of glitch in the matrix.

Then I sent a wire to Luxury Brand Partners, the first big backers. I could hear the faint clack of the keyboard with every zero.

The banker's eyes widened.

"That's the largest wire I've ever done," he said.

I smiled.
"Until now."

I handed him the last wire.
Made out to David and Alexis Thurston.

The climb.
The scars.

The years of saying "not yet" so we could one day say, "hell yes." Now it was ours.

When I got home, I wasn't done. I wrote out checks to stylists who didn't have equity but helped build the brand. One of the checks helped a stylist named Kelly buy her family's first home. She deserved every dollar.

I dropped the checks in the mail. Then hopped on a flight to Paris to see what life looked like on the other side of the wire.

12
PARIS, MOTHERFUCKER

Seventy-two hours after selling Pulp Riot to L'Oréal, I was in a goddamn castle in Chantilly, France.

I'd flown in from Los Angeles.
Alexis flew in from Sweden.
We rendezvoused in Paris.

We splurged on a suite at the Four Seasons George Fifth.
Right off the Champs-Élysées.

Marble floors.
Fresh flowers.
A bed that felt like a cloud made of old money and sin.

L'Oréal sent a black car to pick us up.
No Uber sticker.
No small talk.

It whisked us to the castle, where the global CEO and a few hundred high-ranking execs were mid-conference. We were the surprise finale.

The global president of L'Oréal's professional division, took the mic and said: "In case you haven't heard, we just acquired Pulp Riot."

The crowd, suits and stilettos, erupted.

The lights dimmed.

A sizzle reel began.

A rocket ship jetted across the screen.

Fierce looking models.

Killer product shots.

Instagram numbers climbing like a launch countdown.

Then me on camera, smirking, knocking over boxes of color like dominoes. "We're just getting started," flashed on the screen. Blackout.

"And guess what? The founders are here."

The doors swung open.

Cue Black Eyed Peas:

"I got a feeling... that tonight's gonna be a good night..."

We walked through the crowd.

Hundreds of executives clapped in time with the beat.

Sixty seconds.

Ninety seconds.

Try standing still while the top brass of a $200 billion company applauds like you cured cancer and invented sex in the same week.

I glanced at Alexis.

Her smile said, *Can you believe this shit?*

Before leaving the stage, I said: "We're going to make the L'Oréal execs who bought Pulp Riot look like the smartest people in the industry."

And as we stepped off, I handed the microphone to one of their executives who then complimented Alexis' leather pants and pondered aloud whether he'd look cooler with tattoos like me.

We were founders. Living ones. In an industry that's more corporation than creation; that alone made us legends.

We dined at the castle afterward. Sat at the most prestigious table with the CEO. Photographers chased us across the courtyard. We slipped into the car like shadows. Didn't speak at first. Then we looked at each other, and just fucking laughed.

That was the view from a high step on the spiral staircase. But the air up there gets thin. And the silence? It echoes.

13
THE HONEYMOON

Here's the cliché:
Founder sells company.
Gets rich.
Starts complaining.

But I didn't want to be that guy.
I knew compromises were part of the deal.

To their credit, L'Oréal did a lot right. They hired me a life coach. They introduced me to other founders they'd acquired. They rolled out the red carpet.

David Greenberg and I quickly built a relationship built on trust and integrity. He was a master buffer. He protected our brand. Kept us from getting "L'Oréalized."

He talked. But mostly, he listened. And he left us alone. As long as we crushed our numbers, we stayed in control. And we did.

The company exploded.
I felt seen.
Valued.
For the first time in my career, I felt untouchable.

After years of always feeling like someone was going to come for me, that I might wake up one day and be disrupted; now I finally felt almost invincible.

I had L'Oréal, a $200 billion juggernaut behind me.
It was like becoming a "made man" in the mafia.
Doors opened.
People listened.
No one could fuck with me.

All of the chaos, the risks, the sleepless nights, it felt like we had landed the plane on a private runway. Wheels down. Champagne waiting.

We moved into a beautiful new headquarters; modern, light-filled, creative. I helped design it myself. Every day, I was surrounded by artists and visionaries. Stylists flew in from all over the world to shoot content in our studio.

We weren't just the cool brand with neon hair anymore. We were a global force. And for a while, that was enough.

14
THE HIGH LIFE

I know how this sounds. But stay with me.

I was rich.
Like, really fucking rich.

The kind of rich where you forget what things cost. Where "someday" becomes "right now."

Not only did L'Oréal wire us a boat load of cash. We also negotiated an earn out. Which meant that for each of the next several years, we would get paid a percentage of Pulp Riot sales.

House paid in cash.
Exotic car paid in cash.
Invested in stocks in million-dollar chunks.
I had fuck-you money.
I never had to work again.

We moved out of our 3-bedroom apartment and into a brand-new modern masterpiece. Looked like a cover shoot for Architectural Digest.

I was treated like royalty in the secret corridors of airports. Back and forth, back and forth to Europe. Like a rock star. It was everything I dreamed of. For a while, I floated. Weightless. Unbothered.

But here's the twist no one warns you about: when you get everything you've ever wanted, there's nothing left to chase.

I'd wake up.
Pour coffee.
And think, *is this it?*
Did I really trade the brand I loved for this?

Because by every outside metric, I had arrived. But the high doesn't last. Not in the way you think it will. You get used to it faster than you'd expect.

The new house becomes your normal house. The business class seat becomes just, a seat. The applause fades. And you start wondering, *Is all of this stuff just a clever distraction from the silence underneath?*

I wasn't depressed.
I wasn't spiraling.
But I wasn't climbing either.

I'd spent years climbing the spiral staircase. And now, my foot was reaching upward for the next step and found nothing.

No dragon to slay.
No summit to climb.
Just stillness.

It's a strange thing: to have everything you ever wanted and still feel the pull of something else.

15
THE SLOW CREEP

But when a startup gets acquired by a giant, eventually the friction shows up. Always does.

Things generally slow down.
Approvals can feel like they take forever.
Hiring can become a maze.
Budgets tend to shrink.

Big companies love templates. And they frequently try to apply the old legacy brand templates to fast-growing brands. And this can lead to turning the rocket ship into a rowboat.

They obsess over data. Over profit. Over protection. Even when the top line's soaring, they skip past it to nit-pick the expense report. They forget what made the brand successful in the first place.

Greenberg and many others fought to make it all work, but in a company that size, even well-intentioned shifts can create friction with important relationships, like with distributors, labs, and stylists. After all, let's be real, they were a billion-dollar company, and we were just a scrappy start-up that they were trying to assimilate. One can't expect it to be a flawless transition, or for them to show the same level of concern or be as nimble as we once were.

But it was very difficult. Because I built Pulp Riot on trust, loyalty, and respect. And now I was sitting in meetings while people I didn't know, who hadn't lived the early battles, made calls that could put my relationships at risk and chip away at that trust I fought to build.

But I stayed. I endured. I fought.
But the pressure was immense.

Grow the brand.
Protect the culture.
Keep the peace.
Absorb the blame.
Be the shield.
Be the spark.
Be the adult in the room, and the rebel on stage.

That was the job. That was the weight. Most founders would've tapped out. Maybe I should've. But I didn't. Not yet.

Because through it all, we were still winning.

Two and a half years post-acquisition, Pulp Riot was still the fastest-growing color brand in the professional beauty industry. Every year. No exceptions.

Over a million Instagram followers.
Millions and millions of units sold.
Distributed in over thirty countries.

For the time being, we were defying gravity. But I was really starting to feel the altitude. And it was becoming difficult to breathe.

Even back home, I could feel the drift. I'd built the salon suites next to Butterfly Loft. Poured millions into it. The dream was to give stylists a place to thrive independently. A vision that aligned with everything I believed.

But as Pulp Riot grew, so did my distance. I was in Europe frequently. When I came home, I gave my warmth to my daughters. Then, my Pulp Riot team. Then, my Butterfly Loft team. And there just wasn't enough left of me for anyone else. I couldn't be everywhere at once. I could no longer personally extend my warmth to everyone.

A quiet casualty of growth.

The lease on our salon suites came up. I thought about ending it. But that would've left dozens of stylists without a space. So, at the last minute, I brokered a deal for a salon suite chain to take over.

I didn't make a dime.
I "sold" my salon suites for one bottle of scotch. Really. And they threw in six bottles of pinot noir.
And I got the peace of knowing everyone had a home.

Engineered a soft landing.
Everyone could stay.
But to my surprise, some of the stylists were upset.
Not mad about the new landlord.

Not upset because they had to leave. They didn't.
But because I did.

Another reminder that people don't follow brands, they follow energy.

They wanted my warmth.
But my flame was no longer strong enough.

16
STORM CLOUDS

The Spring of 2020 was a scary time. A full-blown global pandemic. Almost overnight, salons around the world closed their doors.

Butterfly Loft salon was no exception.

We had turned a profit every month since month one.
Ten straight years of success.
And then, nothing.
Stylists were devastated.
Their incomes gone.

I sat in lockdown with a pit in my stomach. Watching the stock market plummet. Wondering how bad it would get. Wondering if anyone was even buying Pulp Riot anymore.

But somewhere in that storm of anxiety, I felt relief. We'd sold our salon suites three months before. We'd sold Pulp Riot almost two years before.

If we hadn't made those moves? I would've been stuck paying rent on the salon suites with zero income coming in. And I would've been paying salaries at Pulp Riot while cash flow dried up.

Forget a high eight-figure payout.

We might've been looking at zero.

We knew we were lucky. And we wanted to help. So, one day early in the lockdown, Alexis and I sat at the kitchen table, pulled out our personal checkbooks and started writing $1,000 checks.

Hundreds of them.

To Butterfly Loft stylists.

Pulp Riot supporters.

The people who helped the rocket ship fly.

We didn't announce it.

We didn't post about it.

We just did it.

But as the weeks dragged on, the mood in the stylist community shifted. They were still out of work. And they were angry.

Some started lashing out at the big companies. Especially L'Oréal.

And then, the hyenas showed up.

Stirring up resentment.

Spreading fear.

Pointing fingers.

Eventually, they turned on Pulp Riot.

And it hit me hard.

We'd built win-win relationships. We'd created opportunities where none existed. We gave artists massive platforms, career launches, and paydays.

And in return, yes, we benefited from their loyalty and reach. But it wasn't a one-way street. It never was.

We'd even just sent hundreds of thousands of dollars to stylists to help during the crisis. None of it mattered.

Instagram had turned toxic.
People were looking for someone to burn.
The world was on fire.
And then, someone decided to throw gasoline on me.

It started with an Instagram Live. Five minutes of rage from someone I didn't know. I was accused of racism. The reason? I hadn't said hello to someone at a packed hair show years before.

That's it. That's all it took. Suddenly, I was trending. Not because of what I built. Not because of what I gave. But because of what I allegedly didn't say in a convention center packed with thousands of people.

Three hundred and seventy-six comments later, I was a villain in someone else's story.

They didn't want truth.
They wanted blood.
And for a moment, I thought they'd get it.

I laid on my bed, blinds closed, phone off.
Couldn't breathe.

Couldn't eat.

Had a ringing in my left ear.

Couldn't stop picturing my entire career going up in smoke. The whole damn climb... a fucking waste.

And here's the part that still stings: Some of the people I had flown out, people I had paid, people I had hugged, spotlighted, mentored, and wrote thousand-dollar checks to just months before went radio silent.

Worse, a few jumped in. Kicked me while I was down. Because calling someone out gets more likes than standing by a friend.

I cracked.

Tears.

Hurt.

And then rage.

But not the kind of rage that burns everything down. The kind that builds.

So, I wrote.

I wrote like my reputation depended on it.

Because it did.

A speech.

A promise.

A war cry.

I stood in front of the camera, and I owned it. Not their version of me, but the truth of who I was. What I believed. I didn't swing back. Instead, I owned up to where our brand fell short, and how we could and should be more inclusive. And what we were going to do about it.

I posted it, and then I disappeared.
I thought it was over.
I thought I was done.
But then something wild happened.
The hyenas started howling a different tune.

I opened Instagram.
Over five hundred comments.
Support from every corner.
Even from former critics.

And the lesson? If you reach for big success, you will attract big haters. But if you build with integrity, the crowd will come back around.

But damn, you better have your allies lined up before the spotlight turns red.

In the end they saved me.
They had my back.

But fuck.
That was dicey.

17
WHEN THE CLIMB STOPS

I'd survived the fire, barely.
But something inside me had burned beyond repair.
I was still showing up.
Still saying the lines.

But the fire behind them?
Barely flickering.

The hair industry had changed.
The energy was different.
The shine was fading.
Stylists were burned out.
Clients were spending less.
Social media was getting louder.
But the engagement was getting weaker.

It was getting harder to break through. Harder to make people care. Harder to feel that electric buzz that once surrounded every launch. Every post. Every show.

The pandemic certainly didn't help. Events got canceled. Education went virtual. Everything felt distant. Remote work took its toll. Our once-vibrant headquarters, the creative war room, turned quiet. No stylists popping by to film. Just Zoom fatigue and Slack pings.

The culture shifted.

Not just at Pulp Riot, but across the whole industry.

The camaraderie.

The defiance.

The art.

It all started to feel transactional.

Less like a revolution, more like a rollout.

And me?

I was getting tired.

Not physically.

Emotionally.

Spiritually.

I was doing the same presentations.

Same trade shows.

Same meetings.

Same cycles.

When you're building something from scratch, everything feels urgent. Electric. But once you've built it, and it's working, it becomes a machine. And you're just another cog.

I wasn't climbing anymore. I was coasting. And I didn't like what that was doing to me.

I was grateful to L'Oréal. Always would be. They gave my family financial freedom. Gave our team global reach.

The hardest part wasn't what L'Oréal changed. It was what success changed in me.

I had climbed the mountain.
I'd built the brand.
I'd won the deal.
I'd hit the numbers.
And then, I kept hitting them.
Year after year.
Show after show.
Meeting after meeting.

I was doing everything right. And I felt nothing. At first, I didn't notice. There were still wins. Still moments that looked like joy. But it wasn't joy. It was performance.

Behind the curtain, I was restless.
Detached.
Bored.
Disoriented.

And slowly, the fire that built Pulp Riot, the thing that made me unstoppable, was barely lit anymore.

To their credit, L'Oréal knew post-acquisition life wasn't all caviar and confetti. So, they hired me a coach.

A life coach.
Named Tracy.
Canadian.
Living in New York.
Sharp dresser.
World-class listener.
Understood L'Oréal.

Understood founders.
Understood me.

We met in person at first, and then we'd been meeting regularly for a while over Zoom. I'd vent about how it seemed like everything moved slower now. How it seemed harder to get things done. How it seemed like I sometimes cared more about Pulp Riot's growth than the company that now owned it.

"I want to hit $75 million this year," I told her.
This would be one of our last meetings.

"Why?" she asked.

I opened my mouth to answer. But nothing came out.

"That made sense before," she said. "But your circumstances have changed. What does your dream version of Pulp Riot look like?"

"Like a rocket ship blazing through space."

"And what does it actually feel like?"

I thought about it for some time before answering.

"I'm feeling like I haven't felt in years, like since I worked my corporate job in San Francisco. I feel, unfulfilled. And I can't figure it out. How can I feel unfulfilled? I got everything on my wish list. Shouldn't I feel full?"

"That's interesting," she said. "Your energy spiked when you imagined your dream. But it dropped the second you returned to reality. Maybe it's because your rocket ship is now weighed down by a few passengers who don't even want to go to space."

That landed deep.

She went on, "I find this all so curious David. You felt unfulfilled with your career in San Francisco, but as you were climbing the staircase you felt fulfilled, even when your product line failed, and even when you had to step back and manage that hair salon."

It hit me.
A revelation.
A secret that changed everything.

My mind drifted.

Tracy broke through the daze, speaking with more force.

"David.
Listen to me.
It's the pursuit.
It's the climb.
That's where fulfillment comes from."

And that's when I realized:
It was time to go.
Not because I was angry. I wasn't.
Not because I was burned out.
But because I was ready.

I had climbed as high as that rocket ship would take me.
And before the engines sputtered, I stepped off the stage.

At the height of Pulp Riot's success. On my terms. While the crowd was still cheering.

18
SIGNING OFF

I posted on Instagram.

"After careful consideration, we've decided to retire from Pulp Riot. We're leaving as it's experiencing record growth, and we're confident it will continue to flourish.

Pulp Riot was an album we wrote. We played it loud, on stages across the globe. But now? We know there's another album in us. We just don't know what it sounds like yet."

Then, I addressed my employees.

"Flying the Pulp Riot rocket ship with you has been the ride of a lifetime.

There was ignition.
Lift-off.
Fire and smoke.
Loud noises.
Shaking.
We thought we might puke.
We thought we might explode.
But we made it.

Now we're detaching from the rocket.
Floating back to Earth.
Grateful.

Blessed.

No idea where we'll land.

But we know it's time."

I logged off my final Zoom call with L'Oréal.

No fanfare.

Just a calendar notification that read:

"Last day, Pulp Riot."

I stared at the screen for a second, then shut the laptop.

Closed the chapter. Literally.

The company that changed my life, gone. The rocket I helped build; someone else was flying it now.

You want to know the weirdest part?

I wasn't sad.

I wasn't even scared.

I felt like a rockstar who just stepped off stage after the biggest show of his life. And instead of partying backstage, I walked out the back door into the alley, lit a cigarette, and looked up at the stars.

Because here's the truth no one tells you: When you sell your company, they throw you a parade. But when you leave, just silence.

They just keep the lights on, keep playing your songs.

Only now it feels like there's a Croatian cover band.

The drummers offbeat.

And someone's added a horn section.

And I get it. That's the deal.

You sell the art; they own the rights.

So, I walked.

Not because I had to.

But because staying would've meant pretending.

Pretending I still had control.

Pretending the mission was still mine.

Pretending I didn't want to start a new fire from scratch.

And as I stepped off the stage, I looked back at the climb. How the hell did I go from managing a salon for $24,000 a year, to selling a hair product company for practically $100 million?

If you had pitched me the story back then, I would've called bullshit.

"David, you're going to create a hair product company."

Okay, plausible.

"You're going to be the founder and CEO of a major color brand."

Sure, buddy.

"And your co-founder will be Alexis, who'll become your wife."

What?

"And you'll sell your company to L'Oréal and achieve financial freedom."

Get the fuck out.

But here I am. And when I look back down the spiral staircase, I see the steps I climbed.

Each one expanding my comfort zone.
Growing my power.
Sharpening my edge.
Every step made me more fearless.
Every step prepared me for the next.

Commitment. Learning. Growing.

Confidence.
Excitement.
Fulfillment.
Discomfort.
Comfort.
Over and over again.

And I can tell you now:
The real tragedy isn't failure.
The real tragedy is not climbing.
Because if I hadn't?
If I'd stayed in my safe job in San Francisco?
I wouldn't just be stuck in a cubicle.
I would have missed all of it.

Alexis.
My daughters.
Butterfly Loft.
Butterfly Circus.
Pulp Riot.

Our home.
Financial freedom.
Helping others.
Changing lives.
Making an impact.

Meaningful relationships with:
Our global community of artists.
Distributors.
Labs.

Performing on stages across the globe.
The stories.
The lessons.
The ride.
All of it... gone.

I was walking away from the title.
The stability.
The salary.
The spotlight.
The role most people would kill for.

Would I regret it?
Maybe.

Would I miss being the boss?
Probably.

Would I be bored?
Alone?
Forgotten?

Maybe.
But maybe not.

People said I was crazy.
"Why leave the best gig of your life?"
Because it stopped being my gig.
Because I don't do nostalgia tours.

Because I didn't like the sound of the goddamn horn section.

19
THE DROP

No meetings.
No deadlines.
No backstage passes.
No stage.
Just space.

The calendar cleared.
The inbox went quiet.

My titles vanished.
Founder.
CEO.
Disruptor.

Just David now.

I didn't realize how much of my identity was tied to the climb.

Who was I if I wasn't building something?
What should I talk about at dinner parties?
What would light me up in the morning?

Success didn't just give me money.
It gave me meaning.

My purpose?
Fading.

People assumed I'd already started my next thing.

Messages rolled in: "What's next?"

I didn't have an answer.

For the first time in a decade, I had no plan. I hadn't reserved the recording studio, because I didn't have any songs that needed writing.

No climb.

Just the drop.

At first, I mistook it for freedom.

But it was something else.

Stillness.

Loss.

Possibility.

Terror.

A blank page can be a beautiful thing. But only if you're ready to pick up the pen. And I wasn't.

Then one morning, in the quiet, Alexis looked at me and said: "Let's get out of here."

20
THE CALM BETWEEN THE STORMS

Alexis and I were in the international terminal at LAX. Destination? South Africa.

We wanted to get away. As far as possible. We wanted quiet. No computers. We wanted to become husband and wife again, not just co-founders.

"Sorry," the agent said at check-in. "You can't board. You need two blank pages in your passport to travel to South Africa."

It felt like the universe had pulled the rug out from under us. We just stood there. Confused. Shell-shocked. Bags packed.

Now what?

One moment, we were soaring. The next, frozen at a ticket counter, grounded by two missing passport pages.

The universe has a way of disrupting even your escape plans. It felt like life wasn't letting us skip ahead. Like it was saying, "Nope. You're not done here. Not yet."

Alexis looked toward the giant destination board, grabbed me by the hand and pointed up. "Where should we go?"

Twenty-four hours later we were in Italy. Sipping espressos on the deck of the Hotel Tremezzo. Watching wooden

Riva boats buzz across Lake Como. Wondering what the hell just happened.

We had no plan.
No itinerary.
Just instinct.

Like vagabonds, we slowly made our way south.
A few days in Florence.
A couple of weeks in Tuscany.
A brief stop in Sorrento.

Finally settling in at the Il San Pietro hotel above Positano.

We eased into a routine of watching the sunset from the hotel's expansive patio, enjoying a pre-dinner glass of wine and a bowl of olives between us. Beside us, Valentino, the Italian fashion designer and icon, nursed a cocktail, as if cast to complete the tableau... Italy distilled into a single frame.

Below us, mega-yachts floated like spaceships on the water.

"I could get used to this," I told Alexis.

Our nervous systems softened. Our ambition relaxed. We were learning to breathe again. And the days stretched on. Our year off unfolded like a slow-moving dream.

Rio. Buenos Aires. London. Paris. Melbourne. Bangkok.

Our eyes softened in photos. My posture uncoiled. Alexis smiled differently, because the world wasn't watching. We were finally living the life we'd earned.

Back when I was running Pulp Riot, I barely slept.
Slack messages at 2 AM.
Every day was electric.

Now?
It was quiet.
Maybe too quiet.

At first, I told myself I needed the rest. That I'd earned it. That the goal was freedom. But freedom without purpose felt hollow.

I'd achieved everything I set out to achieve, yet I felt less alive. I thought freedom was the finish line. But freedom without a mission just made me float.

No weight.
No spark.

I didn't just need to escape something.
I needed to build something.
Something I could shape, own, and protect.
Something with a pulse.

I didn't have any fully formed plan. But in silence, I started wondering if there was a higher step waiting, not freedom instead of a brand, but freedom alongside a brand. Both. Together.

It came in quiet moments. Like staring at the red sand-stone monolith called Uluru, the spiritual heart of Australia, wondering why I felt restless.

Or sitting on a remote island in Thailand, staring out on the turquoise waters of the Andaman Sea, feeling somehow, irrelevant.

I didn't miss the chaos.
I missed the creation.
Missed taking risks.
The electric feeling of an idea taking shape in real time.
The urgency.
The edge.
The rebellion.

But most of all, I missed the people.
The artists.
The late-night brainstorms.
Collaborating.
The community.
The fire.

I missed the way an artist lights up when you give them an opportunity to become something they didn't think was possible. I missed scribbling wild ideas on a white-board at midnight, fueled by the belief that we were building something the world needed, but hadn't seen yet.

I had built a global community. I'd been the center of it. And now, I was just adrift. A nomad.

Eventually, I started talking about it to Alexis. Just what I missed. Never going so far as to admit that I wanted to start another brand. Not yet.

I didn't want to go back and repeat the past.
I wanted to go forward.
Build again.
But do it better.
Cleaner.
Smarter.
More grounded.

I wanted to protect the magic and destroy the bullshit.

To take everything I learned at Pulp Riot:
The wins.
The mistakes.
The philosophies.
The war stories.
Turn them into something that could go even further.

I needed to get back into the recording studio and create a new album.

I had no name.
No concept.
No songs. Not yet.
But I had something brewing inside.
A feeling.
And it was starting to burn.

One year after our spontaneous trip to Italy to step away from the madness, we found ourselves back in Italy to celebrate my birthday.

It was sunset in Venice, the kind that makes you forget time exists. The kind of view that makes you feel like you've won the game of life.

Alexis and I were on the rooftop bar of our hotel. Perched above the Grand Canal. We had Negronis in hand. Blood orange and bitter. Just the way I like it.

Gondolas slipped below us like ghosts.
The sky was blushing.

That's when my phone buzzed.

Text from Stevie:
"Just got released. So did eight others. Had to tell you first."

The calm broke like glass hitting marble. In one message, I could feel the walls of Pulp Riot cracking from the inside.

I looked at Alexis.
She already knew.
Didn't even need to read the text.

We sat in silence, watching the sun drop like a coin in a fountain. Both of us turning the text over in our minds. It felt bigger than a staffing change, like a fault line opening under the brand we'd built.

Up until that moment, we'd held on to a hope that Pulp Riot might stay cool. That our team would keep our vision alive. That Pulp Riot would remain a pillar of our legacy. That years into the future, our daughters could walk into a salon in Australia and see it alive and thriving and be proud of what we built.

When a founder steps away, a brand can still stay true. The crew who built it knows the map. They may chart a slightly different course, but the destination stays recognizable. Take that crew away though, and the compass spins. The brand usually drifts toward something else... maybe all the way from being a movement to being a commodity.

Stevie's text also made us feel a tug of responsibility, for the team we'd left and for the artist community who still believed in us.

As the last of the sunlight faded away, I said what we were both thinking: "I think I need to build again."

Alexis looked at me for a long second. Nodded slowly. "Yeah. Me too."

Cut to New York City.
Weeks later.
L'Oréal HQ.

I arrived after dark. The sleek, modern building was usually buzzing, but now it was quiet. The kind of quiet that made you whisper, even when no one was around.

I checked in with security using my real name, though part of me considered using a fake one, just to keep it off the radar. If someone saw me, it would start rumors. I didn't want to be seen. Not yet.

I stepped into the elevator like a retired athlete sneaking back into the stadium. Not for the cameras. Not for the fans. Just to walk the halls.

I took the elevator up. Found David Greenberg's office. Sat across from the guy who'd once been my corporate shield. The guy who made the call that changed my life.

I thought back to the night, months after we walked away from Pulp Riot, when he flew to Los Angeles to take me to dinner. He didn't have to. He brought a bottle of scotch, told me he wished I'd stayed longer, not just for the brand, but because he loved working with me. That stuck with me. I felt the same way.

We reminisced about the years working together. It wasn't about contracts or market share, it was two people who'd been in the trenches together, clinking glasses as old friends.

It had always been more than business. And that was why I flew for over five hours to New York to talk to him face-to-face.

"I'm building another color brand."

He leaned back.
Eyes wide.
Exhaled.

Then smiled.
"Of course you are."

I didn't dance around it.
"I want to do it in Salon Centric."

He raised an eyebrow.

So, I broke it down. "I'm not trying to hurt anyone. But I'm going to shake things up. You know how this goes, David. We're going to be disruptive. Stylists are going to talk. They're going to switch."

He nodded, listening carefully.

"If Salon Centric carries us, the sales stay in-house. Everyone wins. If not, they'll leave. They'll shop at your competitors."

I paused.

"It's not a threat. It's just reality."

He leaned forward, still smiling.
"I appreciate the clarity."

He said he'd take it upstairs.
Said he understood the stakes.
He said he got it.

Like me, even sounded excited at the possibility of working together again.

Then the call went to Paris.
Paris didn't hesitate.
They slammed the door shut.

No questions. No conversation.
Just a cold, clean "No."

That was all I needed.

Cut to Los Angeles. Back home. Sunset again. I'm on the patio with Alexis. I tell her about how Paris literally blocked our comeback.

She laughs first.
Then I laugh.

Because Paris said no.
Because our team's looking for a new gig.
Because now we have a story.
Now we have our reason.
Now we have our Goliath.
Now the fire's lit.
Now we're definitely doing this.

Because if they wanted me to stay on the sidelines, they should've just let me fade into the Venetian sunset.

But they didn't.
And now the rocket's back on the launchpad.
And this time it's carrying fire.

ACT III
THE CATHEDRAL

21
BURYING THE PAST

If you've ever felt what I felt... that ache when the climb stops. That silence after the applause. That restless feeling knowing that there's more. Then maybe this is your moment too. Because the next act doesn't write itself.

You've got to build it.
From scratch.
With your bare hands.
With your heart full.

No map.
No safety net.
No permission.
Just a spark.
A feeling.
And the guts to chase it.

I'm not done.
And maybe, neither are you.

Let's light the fuse.

During our year off, Alexis and I did everything we could to forget about Pulp Riot. No texts to old colleagues. No checking the Instagram account. We needed space, not just from the brand, but from the entire world that came with it.

But even when you're off the grid, ghosts still find you.

A Salon Centric catalog arrived in the mail. I was flipping through the junk, about to toss it, when I saw it: a full-page ad on the back cover announcing three new vivid shades from Pulp Riot. The vibe was different. I couldn't quite put my finger on it. It was like someone was trying to create in the style of Pulp Riot, but it just missed the mark.

And far worse than that, in our year off we had a relationship crumble.

Right before we left, we'd secured one of our distributors a six-year contract. He had gone all in for us. Hired a sales team. Built trade show booths. Spent real money to build something.

I flew down several times to support him. He was like us. Scrappy. Entrepreneurial. Brave.

One of the other brands he was repping was disruptive to L'Oréal. So, before we left, we gave him some security. Six years of security.

During the year off, we made plans to visit him. He was excited. We were going to go out for a nice dinner. But then a week before we landed, radio silence. No replies. No explanation. Nothing.

Finally, I sent a message: "If I've upset you somehow, I hope you'll tell me. I want to make it right."

Still nothing.

Later I was told that despite us leaving them with what we believed to be a solid agreement, the contract was terminated. Most likely within L'Oréal's rights to do so. But still devastating.

His investment vanished, and so did our friendship. He never said goodbye. That was the worst part.

Deep down inside, we understood that L'Oréal wasn't going to try to steer things off course. They weren't going to try and sabotage things or act out of malice. It was just misalignment. It probably would have happened no matter who bought us.

I feel like the final domino dropped when David Greenberg got promoted. It was a well-deserved move, and I was happy for him. But it meant he was no longer solely focused on professional beauty. He was now overseeing multiple divisions across the entire company.

He was out of the trenches. And with him gone, there was no one left inside the machine who truly understood what we'd built. No one who could say: *This is how we do things at Pulp Riot.*

The promise was: *We won't "L'Oréalize" this brand.*
But, remove me.
Remove Alexis.
Remove Stevie.

Remove Greenberg.

And the promise didn't really stand a chance.

It didn't make us angry.

It just made us quiet.

Because it was our vision.

And now it felt to us like it was being changed.

Before I left Pulp Riot, I gave my replacement a compass. A real one. On the back, I had four words engraved: "Let Right Be Done." It was meant to be his North Star.

Along with the compass, I wrote him a letter. In it, I told him: "In business you must make difficult decisions every day. Often, when choosing between two alternatives most leaders choose the one that will maximize profit the most. But I believe when deciding between alternatives, one should also consider the question, 'What is the right thing to do?' So, if you're looking for Pulp Riot's North Star, it's to sometimes break the rules and to always let right be done."

But slowly, to us, the brand felt like it began to drift from what we intended it to be. The spark felt different. And many inside the community reached out to tell us they could feel it.

So did the people who helped me build Pulp Riot. Stevie, Marisa, Doug, and Kasey, even some of the stylists, one by one, they started getting the words tattooed on their bodies: "Let Right Be Done."

It became more than a slogan.

It became a protest.

A middle finger to what the brand was becoming.

A way of saying:

We remember.

We were there.

We know how things used to be.

Even in paradise, even on the Amalfi Coast or walking the streets of Paris, these moments would creep in. A dull ache behind the adventure.

I noticed that when people talked to me about L'Oréal or Pulp Riot, some interpreted my feelings as mild criticism, others, as praise. The truth lived somewhere in between. My feelings were layered, not black or white. I was a creator who built something from the ground up, watched it evolve into something different, and learned from every moment along the way.

Yes, it was hard watching a company take the brand we created in a different direction than we imagined. But we were also self-aware enough to know they had an entire portfolio of brands to manage, and we didn't have the full picture of how their priorities shaped some of the decisions they made.

I've always been a disruptor, that's part of my DNA, but disruption doesn't come from resentment. It comes from wanting to push things forward, to question what's possible, and to create space for new ideas.

And here is where the nuance comes in. Yes, it became different than what we envisioned, but I still saw L'Oréal as one of the best large companies in the beauty industry. There were incredible people inside its walls, including smart, compassionate leaders who cared deeply about the industry and the artists it served. And to them, I felt no anger, no resentment, only gratitude for the memories and lessons.

And Pulp Riot? While different, I'm not here to judge whether it's better or worse. What matters is that we created something that still employs talented people, supports distributors and labs, and gives artists tools to express themselves creatively. That hasn't changed.

Most importantly, with a little more distance, I could see it clearly: without the change, there may never have been an Act Three. It was instrumental in forming my approach for what I would be creating next.

At the time, we weren't obsessed. We were grateful for the chance to begin again. But at the time, we were healing, because reminders kept showing up. Little cracks in the silence, until we realized we had to face it head on.

It was time to bury the past.

In my home office, the walls were still lined with Pulp Riot relics, like posters from launch events, framed magazine covers from Spain and Ukraine, handwritten letters from stylists, buttons, stickers, t-shirts, Pulp Riot Russian dolls from our Russian distributor.

Each item carried its own weight. Each one was proof that we had mattered. But the chapter was over.

This wasn't a spring cleaning.
It was a funeral.

Box by box, we packed it all away.
Not with anger.
With reverence.
With clarity.

As we sealed the final box and slid it into the back of a closet, I could feel something else stir.

A quiet fire.
A new kind of hunger.
Not to prove anyone wrong.
But to build something right.

"Let's never again create something we'll have to bury," Alexis said, softly.

And that was it.

Ashes to ashes. Dust to dust.
The past was behind us.
And the future was calling.

22
BUILDING SOMETHING DIFFERENT

Let me tell you how the beauty industry really works. Because most people just don't know. I didn't either, not until I was on the inside. So let me pull back the curtain. Let me show you what no one talks about.

The professional beauty world is dominated by just a few multi-billion-dollar corporations. Nearly every major hair color brand you know, they own it. In my opinion, typically, the longer they own a brand, the further they drift away from serving the stylist community. Because, as publicly traded companies, the primary reason they exist is not to serve the stylist, it's to maximize shareholder returns.

One of the top ways they increase their value is by acquiring other brands. Because of this, the professional beauty industry has long been one of consolidation. When you have just a few billion-dollar giants dominating the industry, it makes it difficult, almost impossible, for a new, independent brand to be successful.

So, on the very rare occasion that an indie brand actually breaks through, they get courted and offered a deal which is pretty much too good to refuse. And then they get acquired. That's the cycle.

Now I'm not judging anyone who takes the deal. After all, I did. And looking back, it might have been the right move for that version of us. But there was a tradeoff. We'd sold our life's purpose for cash.

So, we made a quiet vow: this time, we'd build with different intentions. We'd do it our way, or not at all.

This time, we weren't chasing another rocket ship. We were interested in building a cathedral. Not just something that could take off, but something we could live in. Shape. Protect. Something that could last.

A brand we didn't have to sell in order to win.
A brand that *was* the win.

As I thought about building something different though, scattered thought fragments would arrive like weather: quick, uninvited, impossible to sort.

Thoughts about our philosophy...
Maybe the next step wasn't selling.
Maybe it was staying.
Staying in control.
Staying independent.
Staying true.
Not just to build a company, but to make an impact.
To build something that really matters.

There were thoughts about money. Selling can look like a victory, but a rocket ship pays you once. A cathedral pays you for decades. Selling is just trading several years of projected returns for a lump sum now. But if you hold, if you keep building, and you're successful, you collect those returns year after year, and perhaps for decades, while shaping the culture and your legacy the whole time.

There were thoughts about art. Creating and building a brand is a form of art. Thousands of creative choices are made and they all stack together into something singular and alive. I think about David Bowie. He could reinvent himself endlessly because he still owned the music and the persona. He never handed the keys to a boardroom. Why would he? Why would I?

When you sell, you hand over the right to decide what the next verse sounds like. You give strangers the paintbrush.

And there were thoughts about the reality of life. I had lived enough life and knew better than to make promises or to write the future in ink.

What if my dreams change?
What if I get seriously sick?

Burnout happens.
The world changes.
Opportunities come out of nowhere.
Sometimes things stop being fun.
Sometimes life throws punches.
And sometimes, you just want something else.

So, even as we mapped out what the next chapter would be, I held space for uncertainty. After all, how do you build a bold brand around conviction while knowing that your conviction might evolve? That was the tension I lived with.

Because truths don't line up. They circle. Profit and purpose. Freedom and safety. Forever and someday. All of them true. All of them arguing under one roof of thought. This is what it means to build in the gray: to let conviction and doubt share the same breath.

Here's what I did know, and what I could stand behind without hesitation: We'd build it for legacy, as if we'd never sell it. We would build it with love. With clarity. With soul. We'd build something that matters and let the future unfold with honesty.

And when it came time to put pen to paper and map out the early days, it didn't feel like a product drop. It felt like we were preparing the foundation for a magnificent cathedral.

23
THE MANIFESTO

We didn't need to come back.

We had enough money to live out the rest of our lives on a beach in Italy. Sipping espressos. Writing poetry. Ghosting capitalism.

While it sounds like a nice idea, we already knew from experience that lifestyle wouldn't bring lasting happiness.

So, what do you do after you've sold your company? After you've made enough to be free forever? What comes next?

There's no blueprint for what to do after you've already won. No playbook for people like us, the rebels who actually made it.

We'd stood on the highest step we could see. Reached for the next, but there wasn't one. So, to keep climbing, to evolve, we had to build the next step ourselves.

We didn't start with *what* we were going to make. We started with *why* we would create anything at all.

This wouldn't be Pulp Riot 2.0. We had no interest in reliving "the glory days" or running the same play. That would've been safe. Predictable. It probably would have even given us the best chance for success. But it wouldn't have been growth. It wouldn't be climbing.

We loved the community we built with Pulp Riot, and we figured that many of those vivid artists would follow us because we had built trusting relationships with them. So, we decided to start there.

But deep down, we were already dreaming bigger. For us, the next step on the staircase had to be more ambitious. More meaningful. A bigger mountain. A bigger opponent. A bigger impact. A bigger reason to keep climbing.

With Pulp Riot, we were primarily a vivid hair color brand. We had launched more mainstream products, like blonding, toning, and permanent color products, but we were never able to replicate the level of success we had with our vivid colors. Winning in the vivid niche was hard, but winning in the blonding and natural colors space was much harder.

So, to go bigger, to take the next step up, we would set our sights on the heart of the industry and ultimately create a brand where our core emphasis would be blonding and naturals. The mainstream color categories dominated by the fifty-year-old legacy companies, where the founders were gone. The art was gone. And the fire was out.

We wanted to go head-to-head with Goliath and replace the machinery with some much-needed magic.

While those companies obsessed over *what*: ingredients, promotions, and pricing strategies, we would obsess over *why*.

We needed to build our cathedral on solid ground. So, before we named the brand, before we made product, before we told a single soul, we created a manifesto.

We grabbed a pen and wrote down six core beliefs.

1
We believe products are better when they're made in a salon, by stylists

Not in boardrooms, but by Alexis and other artists, in a salon, with gloves on, sleeves rolled.

2
We believe in creating art, not commerce

Most companies find an audience and then try to make something they'll love. We'll just create what we love and trust the right people will feel it.

3
We believe community is the most important thing

Not products. Not profits. Community. If we elevate artists, they'll elevate us. If we make them more successful, we'll succeed.

Our doors will be open to everyone, 500 followers or 500,000. If you believe in us, we'll believe in you. And we'll never work with people who don't align. We've earned that right.

While other companies stay virtual post-COVID, we'll show up. We'll give a damn. We'll never forget who this is for.

4
We believe in people over profits

We'll make the right decision, even if it isn't the most profitable. We'll serve stylists, not shareholders. No spreadsheet will dictate how we treat people. Our mantra will be *Let right be done.*

5
We believe in creating with a high level of quality, craftsmanship, and taste

We'll hold ourselves to a higher standard. Packaging. Formulations. Presentations. Meetings. Events. Tradeshow booths. Emails. Spreadsheets. All of it.

Design will matter. A lot.

6
We believe the glass is half full

In a world full of cynicism, we'll build something different. An optimistic company, full of optimistic people. Missionaries. Not mercenaries. Full of hope and belief that the best is yet to come.

From day one, we knew this wasn't just a hair color company. We were building a platform. A playground. A studio. A space for artists to create, connect, and grow.

We dreamed out loud about doing more. A podcast. A magazine. A fashion line. A film studio. A new genre all together. We dreamed big. About building something that had never been built before.

We decided we would build a company that doesn't just support our lifestyle, but it would become our lifestyle.

Not chase work-life balance.
But work-life fusion instead.
Alignment.

To build a brand that reflected how we live.
A vehicle to blend our business and our values.

To spend days in the recording studio creating what we love with the people we love. To use our resources, our money, energy, time, to build a world we actually want to live in. Full of purpose. Full of joy.

We were blazing a new trail. But in many ways, we were returning to the core of who we've always been.

We believed in artists.
In connection over control.
In building differently.

So, we made ourselves a promise: We would build a company that felt like home. We would build a future that didn't yet exist.

To set the tone, we decided that for several years we'd work without pay. Work, not because we had to, but because we wanted to.

This wasn't just our next act.

This was the next step up the spiral staircase.

And our manifesto was to be the blueprint for our cathedral.

24
LAYING THE FIRST STONE

When Antoni Gaudí began building La Sagrada Família Cathedral in Barcelona, he knew he wouldn't live to see it finished. But he built anyway, stone by stone, decade by decade. A structure designed to endure.

We would do the same. This wasn't just another brand. We were laying the foundation for something more meaningful. A belief system. A new movement. A living work of art. Built slowly, intentionally.

We might not be around to see it completed. But that wasn't the point. The point was to design something worthy of being finished.

And like any cathedral, it started with the right architects.

I took Stevie to lunch at the Four Seasons. Last time we were in the trenches together, we were on a rocket. The Pulp Riot rocket. Fast, wild, and burning white-hot.

Then came the crash.
L'Oréal showed her the door.
No farewell tour.
Just gone.

She didn't get to walk away like I did. Didn't get to trapse around Italy to rediscover herself. She was just cut out of something she helped build. No closure.

I thought maybe she'd be hesitant when I told her we were starting again. But there it was, that unmistakable fire in her eyes.

She stirred her iced tea, reading me. Waiting for the pitch.

"I know what you're thinking," I said. "Another vivid brand. Another Pulp Riot."

She raised an eyebrow. "Isn't it?"

"No," I said.

She tilted her head. "Not vivid?"

I exhaled. "We're not trying to get back what we had. We're going to build something bigger."

I let it hang.

"We're going after Goliath."

That made her pause.

"Blonding. Toning. Permanent color," I continued. "We're stepping into the biggest arena, where the stakes are the highest of all."

She blinked. "You mean... we're going after Redken?"

I nodded. "Redken. Goldwell. Wella. Schwarzkopf. All of the color giants. We're going to play in the big leagues."

She let out a slow whistle.

"That's not a pivot. That's an invasion."

"Exactly."

She leaned back, grinning. "Are you serious?"

I met her eyes. "Dead serious."

And she was in.
Not just in, but ready to burn the whole thing down.

The look in her eyes reminded me of how I felt when Level6 couldn't compete with Goliath, or when Butterfly Loft was disrupted by the Goliath salon suite company.

We weren't just building a brand. We were assembling a resistance. Next came Doug. Marisa. Kasey. Jack. Kris. All tossed aside by L'Oréal. All with something to prove.

I gathered them up.
Gave them equity.
And got to work.
Stone by stone.

First meeting?
Around my glass dining table.
No offices.
No red tape.
No middle managers.

I told them the name:
Danger Jones.

It wasn't just a brand name.
It was a mirror of what I'd become.

Danger - punk rock, tattoos, edge.
Jones - blazer, luxury, precision.

Danger - a vivid brand.
Jones - with sophistication.

Jones - a blonding brand.
Danger - with teeth.

A non-corporate color house with real artistic soul.
Tattooed hands in a tailored suit.
Two worlds, one name.

When I was a teenager, I worked at a record store. I used to stare at the gig posters on the wall and dream of life on tour, city after city, night after night. That dream stayed with me.

So, when it came time to create artwork for our vivid cartons, we hired the same artists who made posters for the biggest bands on the planet.

We told them: "Design concert posters for Danger Jones, as if we were a touring band. Put the venues on them. Put the tour dates on them. No logo. Just art."

The first one came back with a logo on it.

Alexis got pissed off. Fired off an email. "Absolutely no logo. It's art. Not commerce. We're making the music we want to hear."

And that was the vibe.

We weren't creating to appeal to an audience.

We were just trying to become our own favorite band.

Paris shut us out completely.

So we went to their biggest rival: Cosmo Prof.

Salon Centric and Cosmo Prof were by far the two biggest distributors in the United States, and they were locked in a war, competing for a larger share of the market.

We walked in with a playbook they didn't see coming. Not just to win back vivid artists. But to challenge the category that no one could touch. Gloss toners. Those translucent, liquid formulas stylists use to tone, refine, and perfect blondes.

A category dominated by L'Oréal-owned Redken, a color line that was exclusive to Salon Centric. Up until now, they were untouchable.

So, the idea of us pulling blonding and toning stylists from that eco-system? It was fantasy. But it was a fantasy Cosmo Prof couldn't ignore.

They didn't test us.

They didn't tiptoe.

They just waved us through.

Over a thousand stores, on day one.

Over the years, I had built a reputation.

And now I was back with a bigger vision.

Other brands claw their way up for years, even decades.

Most don't even get a meeting with Cosmo Prof.

But not us.

We skipped the ladder.

Took the elevator.

Danger Jones became the first indie color brand ever launched through one of the two distribution giants. And I became one of the only founders in history to create one brand distributed in Salon Centric, and another brand distributed in Cosmo Prof.

We posted it without warning. Months before our launch date. Just a video. Dropped from the sky like a bootleg demo.

It was shot from overhead.

Alexis and I sitting on the floor.

A record player between us.

Albums scattered around.

Prince, Bowie, Stones.

Then, a closeup of vinyl spinning on the turntable.

Danger Jones circling on the center label.

My hand dropping the needle.

Tattooed on my fingers, "Let Right Be Done."

A pointed message to the community.
To Pulp Riot.
To Goliath.

No caption.
Just the words: "Coming soon."

Stylists lost their minds.
They didn't know what it was.
But they knew who it was.
And they were in.

Because people don't follow companies.
They follow people.
They follow beliefs. Values.

Before we shipped a single box, we threw a pre-launch party. Not in a hotel. Not at a club. At our house. That mattered.

Earlier that day, artists painted at our salon. Vivid colors only. Just like the good old days.

They painted all morning. And at night, those models walked a fashion show inside our home. Over a hundred stylists stood shoulder to shoulder, no chairs, no barricades, just two human walls forming a makeshift runway that snaked through the space in a serpentine line. Phones shot up like lighters at a concert.

As the first model turned the corner, vivid hair blazing... the crowd lost it.

They screamed.

They filmed.

They broadcasted it to millions.

The Power of Many was still alive.

The music pulsed.

The models strutted.

And Alexis turned to me and whispered: "I've really missed this community."

The artists hadn't felt this alive in years. And when the last model walked, they turned to us, to Alexis and me, and roared.

Over a hundred stylists flew in.

Not for product education.

Not for sales pitches.

They came to be part of something.

They came for the spark.

To feel the warmth of the flame.

But this time, we weren't just chasing fire.

We were building a structure strong enough to hold it.

25
DANGER FEST

We expected a rocket ship.
What we got was a slow burn.

After launch, the social buzz was electric.
Stylists posted.
Shared.
Tagged.
Our community roared back to life.
It felt like a movement.

But the numbers?
Just okay.
Not bad.
But not great.

We had nailed the vivid formulation, but they didn't move like we thought they would. Not after all that hype. Not after all that build-up.

We had staffed up.
Loaded inventory.
Hit the gas.
But the altitude wasn't matching the fuel burn.

And with our gloss toner launch being just two months away, the real battle, the one against Redken and the other industry giants about to begin, I started to feel it.

That creeping feeling. Not fear, exactly. But concern. And confusion.

We weren't failing yet.
But we weren't flying either.

Was this another Level6? Another failed dream that never lifted off? Or was it another Pulp Riot? Or something else entirely?

During our year off, the landscape shifted. Vivid colors, the category we once ruled, had cooled. Quietly, but undeniably.

We didn't want to believe it. But the signs were everywhere. Labs, distributors, stylists. Consensus was clear, the vivid trend had peaked and was now in a steady decline.

And that wasn't the only shift. The Instagram algorithm had fractured the industry in two: vivid artists and blonding artists. Back in the Pulp Riot days, all types of hair stylists would see our posts. But now, blonding artists were living in a different universe, and we weren't showing up in their feeds.

And yet, we had our vivid community. Loyal. Passionate. Fully engaged. We were grateful for them. They were the spark behind the brand. The heartbeat of the early days. Not just where we came from, but part of who we would always be.

However, a part of me was starting to wonder: Was the old strategy the right one for competing with Goliath?

If we were going to build a cathedral, we had to start with the foundation.

Not product.
Not packaging.
People.

We needed to reignite the stylists who'd carried us before, not to replace them, not to outgrow them, but to walk with them into something new. To show them that the brand they helped build was evolving, not abandoning. That this next chapter could include them, even if it looked different than what came before.

So, we invited them to Mexico. Not to educate. To celebrate. To connect. To remember who we were and show them who we were becoming.

Over a hundred stylists from across North America arrived in Cancún ready for something real.

At check-in: welcome bags, champagne flutes. In the lobby: reunions, tears, Instagram follows turning into IRL friendships. This wasn't a training. This was a homecoming.

Opening night.
Dinner by the pool.

Twelve circular dinner tables.

Tropical linens.

Grilled pineapple.

Caribbean drums.

I raised my glass under the stars. "I want to welcome you home," I said. "But more importantly, I want to show you where we're going next."

The next day, I took to the stage.

No suit. Just truth.

Gave them a transparent look at Danger Jones.

Peeled back the curtain and let them in.

Laughter. Inspiration.

Then I threw a slide up on the screen. "We're not just a vivid brand," it read. Followed it right up with a video teaser of our upcoming gloss toner line. Just two months away from launch.

Then, I clicked to the next slide. A collage of eight dimensional blondes, with depth, shadows, and light all working together, like a million-dollar head of hair. All done by another brand's global ambassador, named Chrissy Danielle, who was one of the most respected blonding artists in the world. The elevated looks were to serve loosely as inspiration for the new Danger Jones look.

"We're not Pulp Riot 2.0," I said. "This time, we're going bigger. Much bigger."

We expected fireworks.

Instead, we got hesitation.

Polite smiles.

Sideways glances.

Not resistance. Just confusion.

For most of them, dimensional blondes and natural colors weren't their jam. We were asking them to speak a language that some of them didn't really speak. And it showed.

They still loved us.

They always had.

But I saw it in their eyes.

I could see my error in judgement.

I'd made a mistake.

This wasn't theirs to carry.

Not because they weren't enough, but because we were asking something that wasn't totally born from their world.

So, I backed off.

Mid-keynote.

Skipped four slides to get back to the familiar.

What they were used to.

Something closer to Pulp Riot 2.0.

Niche. Alternative. Vivid.

That night, Alexis and I sat on the balcony, staring at the ocean. I said, "We'll figure out toners when we get back to LA. But for now, let's show up big for the artists who showed up for us." Alexis nodded.

Danger Fest was a spiritual reset.

During the day:
Poolside collaborations.
Cabana confessions.
Impromptu photoshoots.

At night:
Family dinners.
Barefoot dance parties.
Closing toasts that turned into tears.

Stylists stood up and spoke their hearts.
They talked about identity.
Confidence.
Belonging.

Not one mentioned product.
Instead, they talked about feeling seen.
That's what Danger Jones meant to them.
Not a company.
A mirror.

The CEOs at the goliaths would've thought we were insane. Spending hundreds of thousands of dollars on an event not designed to train or sell, but to elevate.

But this wasn't a marketing spend.
It was a soul investment.

And while the industry watched from afar, plotting, predicting, trying to figure out what we were really up to, we were figuring it out ourselves.

Because in the silence that followed my keynote, I saw it clearly: the vivid community had already given us so much. They were our origin story. Our compass. Our community. And they would always be a big part of the brand's soul.

But if we were going to go bigger, if we were also going to take significant market share from the industry goliaths, if we were going to have a future or lead the next movement, we had to also build something new.

But how?

With just two months until launch, we had no clear plan. Just instincts. And a feeling the path forward wasn't going to look like the one we'd walked before.

Two months after we got back from Mexico, it was time to launch gloss toners.

3... 2... 1... ignition.

Thrusters on.
Lift-off.
The rocket went up.
And then sputtered.
And crashed.

At first, I tried to stay optimistic.
Told myself it was early.
That momentum might build.

But each passing day, the numbers told a different story.

And deep down, I felt it. That weight in my chest.

Pressure.
Doubt.
Déjà vu.
The slow slide to uncertainty.

I'd been here before with Level6.
Was I really repeating the past?

The blonding community didn't know us.
Didn't trust us.
And didn't even see us.

What happened next, would redefine everything.

26
THE MALIBU PIVOT

I could hear the waves crashing below.

I stood barefoot on the deck of a house once owned by Skrillex, a modern masterpiece made of steel, concrete, and glass, clinging to the cliffs of the Pacific Coast.

The infinity pool in front of me spilled over the edge. Disappearing into the foggy morning.

I was going over everything in my head.

How we went from the feeling of winning when we launched in Cosmo Prof, to the feeling of losing as the toners flopped.

Alexis joined me.
Coffee in hand.
Calm as always.

I asked, "What if Pulp Riot was our hit record, and Danger Jones is that follow up album that no one plays twice?"

"We didn't get it wrong," she said. "We just haven't told the full story. And we haven't told it to the right people."

And that's when the fog started to lift.

We had rented the home for a three-day offsite with our leadership team. To them, it probably looked like a retreat. To me, it was a reckoning.

Yes, we were there to talk strategy. But underneath it all, something bigger was shifting.

They sat on an enormous U-shaped sofa. I stood and said what we were all starting to feel.

"We're playing a new game, but we're using the same strategy, even though the rules have shifted under our feet."

The Instagram algorithm had split the industry. Vivid artists were on one frequency. Blonding artists? A completely different one. So, when we posted content for our gloss toner launch. It wasn't reaching the right people.

The product wasn't the problem.
The audience was.

So, I broke it down: "Some people listen to the country music station. Others blast the heavy metal station. But have you ever noticed there's no combination country / heavy metal station? They have two different audiences, with two totally different vibes. So, why are we trying to speak to two different worlds with just one feed?"

The team nodded.
No pushback.

I made the call.
Do something never been done before.

Split the broadcast.

Two Instagram accounts.

One for vivid.

One for blonding.

Two voices, one soul.

If we were going to compete with Goliath in the high stake's world of gloss toners, this is the speed we would need to move at.

We were crossing over to a world that didn't know us. Didn't trust us. Didn't even see us.

In the vivid world, we were legends. But here? We were strangers. The loud kids from the art room trying to sit with the honor roll.

Back in the Pulp Riot days, I knew everyone who mattered. Now, I was scrolling hashtags, finding blonding artists with massive followings and I had no clue who they were.

But we'd been here before. So, we did what we always do. Went back to the basics. We decided to build a blonding community, from scratch. One artist at a time.

Sent DMs.

Shipped product.

No pressure.

Just: "If you like it, let's talk."

Most ignored us.

But some said yes.

We flew them to LA.

Eight at a time.

Created videos where they were the star.

Not the products.

Not the models.

The artists.

Invited them to dinner.

Brought them into our home.

They laughed in our kitchen.

Got a glimpse that we were something different.

It wasn't what they were used to.

It wasn't corporate.

It wasn't just about the product.

It was about how we made them feel.

We invited them into our lives.

Artists started paying attention.

So, we did it again.

Eight more stylists.

More models.

More dinners.

More laughter.

More care.

More trust.

In an industry that had gone quiet since Covid, we were now creating the loudest opportunities.

One of the first artists to say yes was Kylee, from Hawaii. She'd been tagging us, and while she didn't have the biggest following, we noticed something deeper. Her engagement beneath the surface was off the charts. The people who commented on her posts? They were obsessed with her. That's what mattered most to us. Passion, not reach.

At the same time, she was talking to one of the Goliath brands about potential opportunities to work with them. They told her: "Let's talk after your pregnancy."

We took a different approach. "Let's talk now."

We didn't see her pregnancy as a pause button. We saw it as part of her power. So, shortly after she joined our team, we flew her to LA and shot a video of her doing hair with her baby strapped to her chest, wearing a custom Danger Jones onesie.

Then, she and Alexis filmed an interview together, sharing a message you rarely hear in our industry: that working moms don't need to sacrifice their dreams, but in fact, chasing your dreams can inspire your kids.

And then, a short time after Kylee joined our team, it happened out of the blue.

One morning, Chrissy Danielle posted a photo tagging Danger Jones. The artist who I thought was untouchable. The one who created all of the work that was on the mood board I showed in Mexico at Danger Fest.

I interpreted tagging Danger Jones as a sign she was open to talking. So, I reached out.

I learned she'd seen the content.
Felt the vibe.
Watched the movement forming.
Saw how different we were than the corporations.
Liked the edge.
Loved the freedom.
Recognized the opportunity.
And she wanted in.

A couple of months later, Chrissy flew with us to Manchester to teach at her very first Danger Jones education event.

In the front row:
Tia Lambourn.
UK Redken Ambassador.

After the show I boldly walked straight up to Tia and said, "We'll work together someday."

She smiled.
Didn't believe me.
We sent her product.
She didn't want to like it.
But she did.

More importantly, we talked a lot on Zoom. Built a relationship. She loved what we stood for. And a couple of months later, she joined the team too.

And then came Emily Chen, an artist Ambassador from Goldwell who had really made a name for herself, because she was so authentic and real. She generously provided quality education on her social platforms for free, and because of this, she was followed by a ton of adoring fans.

I met her backstage at the Premiere Orlando hair show. We crossed paths as I came off stage and she was heading on to the stage. I said, "I want to get to know you better." She told me to slide into her DMs. So, I did.

We started talking. Almost every day. Zoom after Zoom. It's hard to share what the opportunity is like at Danger Jones when an artist looks at it through the prism of having the experience of working for one of the Goliath brands. She asked hard questions. I gave her honest answers. And soon, Emily took the leap and joined our team.

Kylee, Chrissy, Tia, and Emily weren't just influencers. We connected our circles together, just like the Butterfly Circus team did years earlier. They joined Alexis and I as the faces of our brand. They helped guide the strategy. But more than that, they became our friends. We traveled the world together and created life-long memories. We made each other bigger and better than any of us would be alone.

Suddenly, about a year after the Malibu pivot, everything was different. I could have never envisioned we would go from having no blonding community, to creating a full-fledged blonding movement.

We didn't tiptoe in.
We came in loud.
We left the door open.
And suddenly, everyone wanted in.

And here's the lesson. You don't build a movement by starting at the top. You start by proving yourself where trust is scarce and attention is real.

You create opportunities for the right people.
You treat them well.
You don't buy love, you earn it.
You create relationships where both sides benefit.

That's what we did. We built something real with artists, and the world noticed. Their posts didn't sound like ads. They weren't. They liked our products. They cared about our movement. They valued our community. They were grateful for the opportunities we were providing. And they cared about us as much as we cared about them.

It wasn't transactional. It was human. It was reciprocity. Good people on both ends of the relationship that were united by common beliefs.

It became obvious that if you joined the brand, you weren't just a number. You'd work with the founders. You'd help shape strategy. Sometimes you might fly business class. Sometimes in private jets. Maybe you'd see the world. Or you might help formulate color in Italy. Or cry with us in Mexico.

There's a lesson to be learned, we didn't start at the top of a mountain shouting. We started from the bottom and built a path worth walking. One win led to another, which led to another. Like the guy who started with a red paperclip, traded it up for a fish-shaped pen, then traded it up for a handmade doorknob, and continued trading up until he had a two-story farmhouse. Except we traded belief for trust, trust for loyalty, and loyalty for momentum. One artist at a time.

And there were far more talented artists than the four mentioned in this chapter, who joined our movement, who together made a massive difference. We called them the Balayage Team. They were everything. They posted authentically. They shared without scripts.

They showed we were more than a brand.
Because we were.
We had a mission.
We had soul.
We built community.
We were a movement.

We'd shown that there was finally an alternative to the corporate giants in the blonding space. One that respected their voice. One that elevated their work. One that moved with them, not above them. They're why we do this.

The gloss toner movement didn't just bring in sales. It brought in belief. Distributors started paying more attention. Stylists who'd never used vivid were now entering our world through blonding & toning.

It changed the energy in the company. The vibe at shows. The way we walked into rooms. Because when you finally hit product-market-community fit? Everything shifts.

Gloss toners quickly became our flagship.
We had the right product.
The right story.
And now we had the right community.

We didn't just break into their world.
We built a new one.

The Malibu Pivot wasn't just a strategy. It was a spiritual return. We'd stumbled hard, adapted, innovated, and climbed. And now, the staircase was turning upward, and fast.

We didn't just rebuild a community. We tapped into something bigger. A force we'd used before, but never at this magnitude: The Power of Many.

27
THE POWER OF MANY

Every brand needs a secret weapon. This is ours.

Not a formula.
Not a budget.
A belief system.

It's The Power of Many.

It started at Butterfly Loft.

I taught our stylists how to be better at Instagram, not just to scroll, but to broadcast. We went from marketing the salon to Los Angeles to reaching the world. Our stylists won. We won.

Then came Butterfly Circus.

Me and several influential stylists across North America linked our circles together to create a touring education team. The stylists won. We won.

Then, at Pulp Riot, it scaled.

Stylists carried our message, filled our feeds, and pushed our products into the spotlight, and in return they gained real value: community, income, opportunities to gain notoriety and work with a brand they love. We all won.

And now, with Danger Jones, we've taken it further than ever before. Every time we launch a product, we send out 500 curated promo boxes. No contracts. No paid posts. Just a box, a belief, and a stylist with a phone.

And then, boom.
The stories start flooding in.
Unboxings. Tears. Laughter. Shock.
It's raw.
It's real.

We don't script a thing. We just give them something worth talking about. Because when it's real, they believe, and they want to share it, because it's their brand too. They know that if they help us grow, we will have more opportunities to help them grow.

When we throw a fashion show in our living room, they light it up online. When we dance by the sea at Danger Fest, they broadcast it.

Not just to show off, but to show others what's possible. This isn't a marketing tactic or an influencer campaign. It's a movement of believers.

It's never been formal. But it's always been clear. We give stylists tools. Visibility. The chance to turn talent into influence. Side gigs into careers. And everyday color into art that moves people.

We hand them the mic.
Give them a stage.
Turn on the spotlight so they can shine.

It's not about us paying artists to pretend they love us.
It's about empowering artists who already do.

Because here's the truth:
Independence gives us freedom.
But interdependence gives us flight.

It's not just about breaking away.
It's about rising together.
We elevate them.
They elevate us.

And that's how you build something that can't be replicated. This is how you beat giants.

Not by swinging harder.
You don't do it alone.
You get more people to swing with you.
That's the revolution.

One day I had a thought: If our community is this powerful, what would happen if we linked arms with other brands?

So, I picked up the phone. Called leaders from a few of the brands who seemed to get community, and I pitched something no one in our space was doing. Let's stop acting like competitors. Let's collaborate. Let's create shows where our communities collide.

Let's share the stage.
Share the spotlight.

Share the fans.
Link our circles together and win together.

And they said yes.

In a world of egos and guarded turf, we created something rare: alignment.

So why don't most of the big brands do this?
Ego.
Control.
Fear of losing the spotlight.

Most treat stylists like ad space.
We treat stylists like co-creators.

They build hierarchies.
We build circles.

Most leaders want to be the genius in the room. I just want to connect the right people and make the room magic.

Stylists feel the difference.
That's why they show up.
That's why they stay.

If I have one gift, this is it: I know how to bring people together. Stylists. Educators. Brands. Outsiders.

I know how to spot the spark.
How to pour gasoline on it.
How to turn a whisper into a roar.

Because when you unite the right people around a common belief? It stops being your story. It becomes *our* story.

And that's how we win.
Not once.
Not twice.
But over and over again.

28
CATCHING FIRE

It started as a spark, and then it spread.

Distributors came to us, from all over the world. Drawn to this strange new brand from Los Angeles. They reached out, wanting to know what all of the buzz was about.

While other CEOs were asleep, I was often in my kitchen at 4 AM. Barefoot. Coffee by my side. Zoom camera on. Telling the story of Danger Jones to a distributor in another time zone.

They expected me to talk about products, but I talked about purpose. They expected me to lead with science, but I led with soul.

I told them why our packaging looked like gig posters. Why our products were made inside a working salon. Why we believed that people matter more than profit. Why art matters to us more than commerce. Why speed, community, and authenticity can beat Goliath.

Why. Why. And more why.

And I saw it happen again and again, curiosity turning to fire in their eyes. Because it turned out that my Goliath was their Goliath too.

Zoom calls started turning into plane tickets. And soon, Alexis and I were everywhere. London, Sydney, Paris, Dusseldorf, Taipei, Milan, Warsaw. And on and on and on.

City after city.
Event after event.
Every trip a blur of press interviews.
Stylist gatherings.
Stage shows.
Late-night toasts.

We traveled like a band on tour. Tired. Jet-lagged. Lit up from the inside.

I'd open my phone and see signs it was working. Stylists broadcasting about Danger Jones in Dubai, or in Reykjavik. Our art, our tone, our spirit, echoing around the world.

In just 23 months, Danger Jones already had distribution in 43 countries.

23 months.
That number meant something.

Because 23 months was how long it took us to launch and sell Pulp Riot.

This was the mirror moment.
Two brands.

Same founder.
Different fates.

Danger Jones was taking off.
And Pulp Riot? It was changing.

While Danger Jones grew to 43 countries, Pulp Riot pulled out of most of the countries it was in. For some reason they appeared to shift their strategy toward focusing primarily on North America instead.

Stylists started reaching out:
"It feels different."
"It doesn't hit the same."
"What happened?"

Sometimes, when a brand changes hands, the heart doesn't always transfer with it. It becomes something else. Not better. Not worse. Just, different. And sometimes that difference is felt more deeply than anyone expected.

In acquisitions, sometimes squeezing the margins can lead to losing the magic. Same goes for running a passion brand with a legacy playbook. Or changing formulations. Or moving headquarters. Or outsourcing marketing.

It's not sabotage.
It's not malice.
It's more like misalignment.

It happens too often in acquisitions to be just coincidence. Over time, the fire that once burns so bright... it changes.

The sound of something catching fire:
At first, it's quiet.
Just a flicker.
A feeling.
A different tone in the comments.

Then it grows.

Stylists post without being asked. Other brands want to collaborate. You land in a city you've never visited, and they already know your name.

That's not marketing.
That's momentum.

It doesn't explode all at once.
It builds.
One post.
One artist.
One conversion.

Then another. And another.
Until it's not a product launch.
It's a movement.

A cathedral taking shape.

29
THE NOMADIC CEO

On a recent morning, we were having a coffee and croissant at the airport in Tallinn, Estonia. A sign on the wall caught my eye. It read, "Anticipation is the best part of travel."

It probably is for most people. They book their flight months in advance. Count down the days. Their whole year builds to a two-week escape.

I sipped my coffee and dug deep into my memories. I could kind of remember what that was like. Just kind of. They're good feelings that I sometimes miss having, but my life is different now.

Most CEOs work from an office. Mine is a window seat at 35,000 feet, watching the curvature of the earth as we pass over Greenland.

Over the last two years, Alexis and I have lived in motion. Not for leisure, but for legacy.

LA.
London.
Hong Kong.
Sydney.

World class cities.

Four different continents.

All in one week.

A month prior, nine hotels in thirty-three days.

Trains cutting across Europe.

Pre-dawn landings.

Not for vacation.

For impact.

This isn't just the job.

This is my life.

At the airport, we move through security with fluid movements. Like choreography. Muscle memory.

This is the rhythm now.

Hotels.

To SUVs.

To airports.

To lounges.

To Boeing 787s

To shows.

Repeat.

I take a photo of my hotel room number, so I won't forget it. The suits in business class glance at my tattoos. I don't look like the rest.

Sometimes I wake up and forget what country I'm in. Sometimes I stare out the window and feel like I'm in a dream. And tonight, I order the second glass of pinot noir at altitude, because when the cabin lights dim and you're in the quiet hush of a midnight flight, sometimes it seems to hit just right.

30
THE HIGHER STEP

Alexis is asleep right next to me.
Creative partner.
Life partner.
Row mate in seat 2B.

Her notebook is open, and so is mine. Hers filled with color. Mine with ideas. Together they tell the whole story, science and spirit, form and fire.

I feel at peace, knowing Stevie's steering the ship back in Los Angeles. Because we'd successfully moved from *Danger* to *Jones*. From chaos to clarity. From rebellion to rhythm. Two halves finally in sync.

I think back to the first climb... to Pulp Riot. Back then, I thought the top step of the spiral staircase was to sell. That's what success looked like. That's what everyone aimed for. That's what all the books said. So, that's what I did. I traded the brand for money and lost the magic.

I had a brand, but no freedom.

Then came the year off.
Adventures without stakes.
Days without meaning.
No climb.

I had freedom, but no brand.

Outside the window, the world curves gently toward dawn. I feel still enough to understand what all this motion has been trying to tell me. I can finally see it. I had committed to building Danger Jones without a clear view of what the next step would be. My foot had been searching in the dark, reaching for something solid. Now, I can feel the step under me.

The higher step isn't brand OR freedom.

It's brand AND freedom.

Creative control.
Cultural impact.
Artistic integrity.
Entrepreneurial power.

That's the game I'm playing.
That's the life I'm building.

This is the higher step I couldn't see before.
And now that I've found it, I can't unsee it.

Because now, I feel a harmony between what I build and how I live.

I'm not trading brand for freedom, or freedom for brand.

I'm choosing both.
Brand and freedom.
Art and life.
Danger and Jones.
Every single day.

This isn't always easy.
But it's the life I chose.
I've built a new rhythm.
A life where the ground is always moving.
But the direction is up.

From the outside, it might look like I'm drifting. But I've never been more grounded in who I am. What I want. And where I'm going.

It might look chaotic.
But from 35,000 feet, I can see the pattern.
The staircase spirals upward.
And I'm right where I'm supposed to be.
Still climbing.

31
THE GRIND BEHIND THE GLAMOUR

When you're the face of the brand, you don't get to coast.

Every city, I'm on.
Every show, I'm in focus.
Every room, I'm seen.

In every moment, I've got to be the most charming person in the room. Jetlag doesn't matter. Time zones don't excuse me.

They only know I showed up.
And that matters.

After the event, I don't disappear backstage.
I go into the crowd.
Shake hands.
Take selfies.
Remember names.

Because I love these people.
I'm grateful for them.
And because that's the job.

They see me traveling the world. They don't see the red eye from Tokyo, the missed connection in Frankfurt, or the midnight cab ride to a hotel that smells like bleach and regret.

They see the fire onstage.

They don't see me pacing the room in silence.

Rewriting every line of my talk on the hotel notepad.

Again. And again. And again.

Until the rhythm feels right.

They see the freedom.

They don't see the calendar that never ends.

The 4 a.m. Zooms.

The midnight follow-ups.

The pressure of showing up.

Even when I'm cracked open and running on fumes.

They see the charisma. They don't see the nights I question everything. The mornings I wonder if I'm too tired to keep going. The flights where I close my eyes and whisper, "Just hold it together."

They see the brand.

The movement.

The myth.

But I'm still the guy who laces up my own gloves before the fight. Who rewrites the pitch deck until the last slide sings. Who shows up early, listens hard, and answers every message from a stylist in New Zealand like it matters. Because it does.

They think I'm fearless.

But I'm not.

I'm just willing to walk into the fire.

Without a guarantee.

They see highlight reels.
They don't see the repetition.

They see results.
They don't see the rituals.

They see arrival.
They don't see the climb.

Because this isn't about magic.
It's about mastery.
And mastery is boring.
It's quiet.

It's showing up when the cameras are off.
When no one's clapping.
When no one's watching.

They see the dream.
But the dream costs something.

And most people want the life without the work.

The freedom without the grind.

The win without the weight.

So, if you're looking for the secret, this is it:
Live the discipline.

Even when no one sees it.
Especially then.

Because this... this is how you build a cathedral.

32
UNIFYING THE INDUSTRY

One year after Danger Fest, we arrived back in Mexico. Second year. Same resort. But this time, it felt different.

Twelve months ago, we couldn't even get a blonding artist to open our DMs. Now? Pretty much half the crowd was from the blonding side. And they weren't just there to listen. They were all in.

On night one:
The blonding crew and the vivid crew sat at opposite sides of the dinner table. Guarded.

By the end of the weekend:
They were shoulder to shoulder.
Laughing.
Crying.
Taking shots.
Trading formulas.

It was working.
We were unifying the beauty community.
Two worlds becoming one.

The next morning, they filed into the convention hall. The same one where I delivered the gloss toner speech the previous year, the one that didn't land the way I had hoped.

Alexis and I stood in the back. Behind closed doors. Waiting for our entrance.

The countdown lit up the screen.
Five minutes.
Then four.

TLC's "Scrubs" was blasting through the room. The entire crowd was singing along. Word for word. They were primed.

Then... silence.
A glitch.
The audio had cut out.

I looked at Alexis. "Shit. They just killed the moment."

But then, out of the silence, something happened.

The voices kept going.
On their own.
Like a chorus.
No music.
No cue.

More than a hundred stylists, jetlagged and wrung out. Filling the room, singing in unison, acapella, with no backing track.

It wasn't a song anymore.
It was a signal.
We're in this together.

Then the music kicked back in.
And the countdown hit zero.

A giant phone filled the big screen.

Inside it, a reel played.

It showed stylists at our house.

On our stages.

Backstage at shows.

Filming content at Butterfly Loft.

Dancing at our parties.

Walking through airports.

Hugging in hotel lobbies.

Then the sizzle reel exploded.

Rapid-fire clips.

Forty-three countries.

Ninety-two products,

180 artists we worked with.

All in just two years.

Then it flashed across the screen:

"Welcome the Founders. David and Alexis."

The doors opened.

The music pulsed.

They stood.

Cheered.

Clapped to the beat.

We floated down the aisle.

These weren't customers.

They were our people.

We didn't just build this community.

We belonged to it.

When I took the stage, I spoke from the heart. Shared the highs, the bruises, and the future. Totally transparent. It was *our* brand, after all. Announced permanent color. Made them feel it.

Then came the speeches.
Eight artists.
Ten minutes each.
Raw, emotional, vulnerable.

One artist shared her story of addiction, recovery, and how we helped give her life meaning again. Others followed, talking about being seen, having a shot, finding their people.

The theme was clear:
This brand didn't just change their careers.
It opened doors.
Gave opportunities.
Provided meaning.
Changed their lives.

I cried.
So did everyone else.
Because this is what impact looks like.
Not a metric.
Not a sell-through rate.
It's about lives changed.

Recently an artist thanked me, not only for bringing a new circle of friends into her life, but also for making it possible for their children becoming friends too.

They fly across the country for each other's birthdays. Get Danger Jones tattoos. Make their own merch. Post quotes from my speeches. Send us DM's that still break us open.

Every event we throw, whether it's a launch, a training, or a party, is engineered not just to educate and inspire, but to gather. To reconnect our crew. To pull people closer.

A stylist posts from our event.
Her audience sees it.
Someone gets curious.
They try the product.
They feel the shift.
They tell a friend.

I used to want to make a big splash.
Now I care more about creating a million ripples.
Because ripples become waves.
And waves become currents.

We've turned stylists into educators. Educators into travelers. Artists into believers. We remind them why they fell in love with hair in the first place.

Distributors tell us they feel alive again. Former corporate execs walk away from the Goliath companies to join our team, to become a part of something real. Even competitors have changed how they move. They're watching closely.

This is the life we wanted:
Events that feel like festivals.
Days filled with connection.
Nights filled with meaning. A life that feeds us emotionally, creatively, and spiritually.

Danger Jones is the platform.
But the real product?
Possibility.

And the ripple effect?
It's only just begun.

So, if you're building something, ask yourself:
Are you chasing followers, or forging bonds?

Followers scroll.
Bonds stay up late.

Bonds get on planes, hop time zones, and sing when the music cuts out.

33
THE NEXT WAVE

After you light the fire, after the pivot works, after the movement begins, what then? You find yourself staring not at a finish line, but at a blank page.

This is where most memoirs end. But I'm not writing a memoir. It's a manifesto for a new way of building, and the cathedral I'm building is still taking form.

Now we're in uncharted waters.
More countries.
Bigger partners.
More eyes.
More temptation to play it safe.

But we're not here to play it safe.
We're here to build something that lasts.
And that's what the next wave is.

It begins with the most daring creation yet: Epilogue. Eighty-four shades of permanent color. The "family farm" of the legacy brands. The category that pays all of their bills.

So, we flew to Milan several times. Brought several stylists with us. Spent many focused days inside one of our labs.

By the day, they tested formulas on live models, under controlled lighting. I watched them stand shoulder to shoulder with the chemists, studying every nuance, tone, undertone, and reflection.

We drank wine at night. Laughed hard. But make no mistake, we were crafting a weapon. One that could take on Goliath. And perhaps win.

But first, we needed shelf space. So, we boarded a private jet. A Challenger 350. And flew to Denton, Texas, to pitch Epilogue to Cosmo Prof's executive team.

It was Stevie's first time flying private. She worked through the entire flight. At one point, she looked up, smiled: "Better than working at Starbucks."

We laughed. Because we'd come a long way from folding towels at Butterfly Loft, and from bootstrapping Pulp Riot, to flying at 35,000 feet to pitch billion-dollar partners.

But this wasn't about luxury. I rarely spend money on luxury anymore. I spend it to make an impact. You see, we were flying into the belly of the beast, carrying hope that we were going to shift the trajectory of the industry.

We walked into a boardroom.
Long conference table.
Screens glowing.
CEO present.

They didn't know the name yet.
Didn't know the look.
Just knew we wanted a lot of shelf space.

They were skeptical.
Ready to dismiss us.

That's when I do my best work.
I tell the truth.
I light the fire.
I make them believe.

I dropped the teaser video. Unveiled the packaging: white-on-white, debossed, edgy luxury. Clean lines. Zero clutter. It didn't just stand out; it made everything else look outdated.

They sat up.
They leaned in.
They saw what we saw.

We had evolved. We were no longer a scrappy new-comer. We had become a serious global alternative to the big corporations.

We walked out with shelf space.
Belief.
Momentum.

On the flight home, we opened a bottle of wine and ate Texas barbecue high in the sky. Not to celebrate ourselves, but the movement we were building.

Epilogue isn't the end.
It's the start of the next wave.
And the wave's getting bigger.

Right now, as this book goes to print, we're in the middle of something big. We're crafting the launch campaign for Epilogue. While the corporate brands have started hiring celebrities with no connection to our world to be their global ambassadors, and the faces of their campaigns, we're putting our artists front and center.

Not models.

Not actresses.

Not influencers from outside our industry.

We're handing the mic to Chrissy, Kylee, Tia, and Emily. They've walked beside us through this journey. And now, they're going to be the faces of the Epilogue campaign.

Will Epilogue be successful? We think so. But the truth is, we're still in it. Still building. Still figuring it out as we go. We committed, and now we're in that messy learning stage of the Commitment Cycle, a place where I've become more comfortable living inside of.

And what about our vivid artists? It turns out that our vivid colors remain strong... stronger than I expected. The artists who built the movement with us are still here: showing up at every event, flooding our feeds with their fearless work, reminding me that vivid isn't a trend to outgrow, but a language that keeps evolving.

While other brands have quietly stepped back from the vivid category, we've stayed committed. Trends in beauty are like tides; they rise, recede, and rise again. I don't believe vivids have peaked for good. The pendulum will swing back, and when it does, we'll be right here, stronger than ever.

Vivid color isn't just a product line for us. It's part of our DNA, and the community that surrounds it will always be a permanent, essential piece of the brand we're building, together.

Danger Jones is evolving, which means that I'm still climbing. We're not just building a hair color brand. We're building a *creative* brand, where anything is possible.

This year alone, we're releasing three feature-length rock documentaries under the Danger Jones name. These aren't side projects. They're strategic extensions of the same mission. And we expect it will turn Danger Jones into a cultural force that lives beyond the salon chair.

They're all part of the same creative universe we're building, and we call it the "Dangerverse".

They're expressions of our ethos. Storytelling. Disruption. Community. And culture that transcends industries.

The first - A film about the legendary hotel in Hollywood called the Sunset Marquis. Yes, it's a hotel, but it's really about something deeper. It's about a hidden corner of Sunset Boulevard that became a sanctuary for rebellion, collaboration, and creative magic. It's not just a setting, it's a place that's become a community full of rock stars, like Bruce Springsteen, Slash, Simon Le Bon, Morrissey, Dave Grohl, Billy Bob Thornton (all are in our movie). At Danger Jones, that's what we've built too... a sanctuary and a global community of artists.

The second - A film about the iconic alternative radio station called KROQ. They didn't just play music. They created movements. And they turned a lot of artists into stars. They helped break bands like U2. No Doubt. Green Day. Depeche Mode. And in our own way, we do the same. When we see an artist with a spark, we fan the flames until they light up the room.

The third - A film about a band called The Black Crowes. A band that never chased trends. Never pandered. They didn't care so much about commercial success, they just wanted to make the music that sounded good to them. At Danger Jones we take the same approach. We're just trying to write songs that sound good to us.

And maybe, just maybe, this is only the beginning.
What if we thought bigger. Much bigger.

I'm sharing these next ideas, not because they're all guaranteed to happen, but because they show the way I think-expansively, playfully, and without limits. This is how you build not just a company, but a world.

Perhaps... *The House of Danger.*
A stylish office space that encourages collaboration.

Part salon. Part content studio. Apartments above carefully curated for stylists. A screening room for our films. And a bar where every night feels like Danger Fest.

A pod for builders, rebels, and visionaries. A place where my daughters might work one day. Built not just to scale, but to endure. To matter.

Or... *Danger Pad.*
A vacation home where artists could retreat, reconnect, and dream. Maybe in Turks and Caicos. Salt air. Bare feet. Big ideas.

Maybe... *Danger Jet.*
Black exterior. White logo. So, we can show up anywhere and make an even bigger impact on our artist community.

Or perhaps... *Danger Villa.*
Live part-time in Italy. Close to our labs, our distributors, and our international artists. Invite stylists to stay there to get away and be part of the creative formulation process.

Because the goal isn't to build a company.
It's to build a world.
One I want to live in.
And one that's open to everyone I care about.

If it all sounds over the top. Good.
I'm not here to play it small.
I'm not going to stop dreaming big now.

I've got more steps to climb.
This isn't the end of the story.
It's the start of the next wave.

And this wave?

It's just beginning to rise.

34
THE MYTH OF ARRIVAL

They don't tell you this part.
The finish line is a mirage.

"Making it" doesn't mean feeling like you've made it. No number, no view, no title ever really quiets the hunger.

You think if you just get there.
The bank account. The exit.
The house. The jet.
You'll finally exhale.

But what I've learned is this: the most dangerous lie success tells you is that you're done.

That's when people start shrinking.
Start protecting instead of building.
Start repeating instead of risking.
They arrive and forget how to climb.

Not me.

I've seen what's at the top.
And I've chosen to keep moving.
Not because I'm unsatisfied.
But because I'm alive.

So, if you're chasing some future where everything is finally calm. Finally perfect. Finally enough.

Be careful.

That place doesn't exist.

35
THE SPIRAL CONTINUES

I don't believe in arrival anymore.
There is no final curtain call.

I believe in evolution.
I believe in the spiral.
Not just taking me higher but pulling me deeper.
Into the work.
Into the learning.
Into myself.

Each turn of the spiral teaches you something new.

You build something real.
You burn something down.
You begin again.
And then, you rise.
Not to the top, but to the truth.

That's been my path.

Leave the corporate world.
Fall flat.
Build again.
Win big.
Walk away.
Start over.

Each step looked like a different journey. But they were all part of the same climb. Not a straight shot to the top, but a winding staircase inward.

Every step brought me closer.
Not to a destination.
But to myself.

And now, I'm here.
On a higher step.
Not done.
Not even close.

Still climbing.
Still hungry.
Still becoming.
Deeper.
More grounded.
More intentional.

I'm no longer chasing success like it's something outside of me. Now, I see it as something I live.

Danger Jones isn't a brand I'm trying to escape from. It's the vehicle for the life I want to live. It's the platform for the values I want to share. It's the way I leave my mark.

And that impact doesn't end with me. It lives in the stylist who dares to dream bigger. The one who opens a salon. Or builds their own brand.

In the artist who finally feels seen. In the entrepreneur who feels, *I'm done playing small.*

It lives in anyone who's ever had a vision and wondered if they were crazy for chasing it. Anyone who's felt stuck in a system that doesn't fit. Anyone who's burned out, broken down, or ready to begin.

And it lives in the reader who finishes this book and finally says: "I'm ready to start."

Danger Jones is a cathedral that's being built.
Every choice, every risk, every long night.
It's all stone and stained glass.

Built to elevate.
To last.
To mean something.

It started with a ripple.
Became a wave.
Then a current.
And now?
Now it's pulling me forward.
Not toward a finish line.
But into what's next.
Whatever that may be.

Commit.
Learn.
Grow.
Confidence.
Commit again.
Climb.

EPILOGUE

Maybe you picked up this book because you love business. Or because you've been burned by it.

Maybe you're chasing something.
A dream. A number. A name.

Or maybe you're trying to remember who you were before the world told you to play it safe.

I wrote this book because I've lived it.

The rise.
The silence.
The return.

I've sold the company.
Bought back my time.
Tasted luxury.
Faced the void.

And then chose to start again, not because I had to. But because I couldn't not.

What I've learned is this:

Committing is everything. It's the moment the story begins.

A beautiful life is crafted, not stumbled into.

The power of many will always outshine the illusion of one.

Your Goliath, whatever that may be, can be defeated.

You can build a life of freedom *and* have the brand.
And it's worth every scar.

Dream so big, it almost feels foolish.

And there's always a higher step, but sometimes, you have to climb inward to reach it.

If you've been waiting for a sign, this is it.
You're not too late.
You're not too broken.
You're not too small.

Start where you are.
Commit.
Light the match.
And build something the worlds never seen.

You don't need millions.
You don't need permission.
You just need a reason.
And the guts to follow it when it calls.

This isn't a victory lap.
It's a new playbook.
For the rebels, the artists, the builders, the believers.
It's not a book about building a brand.
It's a manifesto about building a new way to live.

That's not just what this book is about.

It's what Danger Jones is about.

And it's what I'm still about.

Even now.

Notebook open.

Jet humming underfoot.

Wheels just leaving the ground.

Alexis' color-stained hands in mine.

The cabin lights dim.

The sky outside turns gold.

And my mind drifts.

Not to what's behind us.

But to what's ahead.

Because no matter how far I've come, no matter what I've built, sold, or walked away from, the spiral continues.

And I'm still climbing.

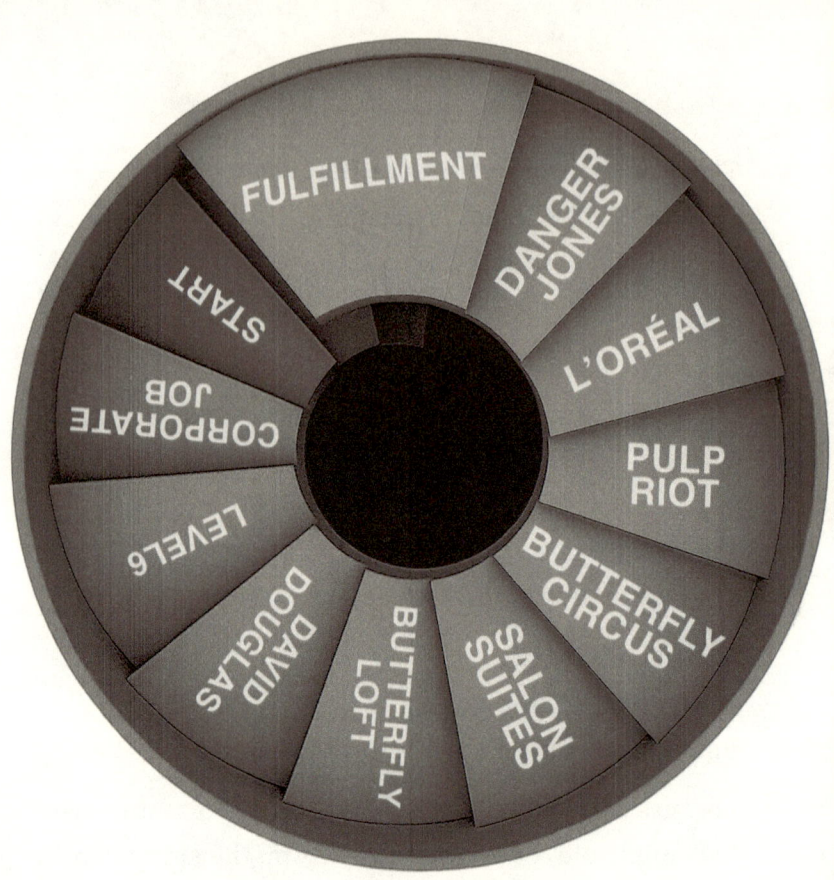

Each step looked like a different journey.
But they were all part of the same climb.
Not a straight shot to the top.
But a winding staircase inward.

Every step brought me closer.
Not to a destination.
But to myself.

NOTES FROM

THE CLIMB

-A DEEPER DIVE INTO 10 LESSONS FROM THIS BOOK-

NOTE 1
THE POWER OF MANY

**How to work with others so you all grow
faster and bigger than you ever could alone**

Let me tell you something that took me too long to learn... you don't win alone.

If you're building a brand, a career, or a movement, and you're doing it in isolation, you're leaving power on the table.

The turning point for me came when I stopped chasing solo success and started connecting circles. Instead of just growing my audience, I started asking: Who else is building something great? And how can we link up and rise together?

The Power of Many took my career into hyperdrive. During the Butterfly Circus era, our little team of artists could work together to get a message out farther and faster than the billion-dollar brands, and that network helped launch Pulp Riot into the stratosphere.

How do you turn collaboration into an advantage?
Here's how:

1. Start with alignment, not numbers.

Don't chase people with the biggest followings. Find people who believe what you believe, whose values, energy, and intentions align. Belief is more powerful than reach.

2. Link your circles.

Each of you has an audience. A following. A network. When you post together, tour together, or launch something together, you create crossover. Your audience finds them. Theirs finds you. It creates compound influence, fast.

3. Split everything fairly.

Credit. Revenue. Opportunities. Ego kills movements. Generosity fuels them. If you want people to go the distance with you, make sure they're eating well along the way.

4. Create moments worth broadcasting.

Make it feel like an event, even if it's just a post. Do something bold. Unscripted. Emotional. When its real, people want to share it. And when the message spreads? Everyone involved gets elevated.

5. Keep it messy and human.

The most powerful collaborations don't come from contracts. They come from group texts. Late-night ideas. Real friendships. The moment it becomes too corporate, it loses the magic.

When it works, it's not just about exposure.
It's about belief spreading at scale.

That's how movements form. That's how careers are made. And that's how you get a message out to the world, not as one voice screaming into the void, but as a chorus.

You want to go far?
Go together.

NOTE 2
THE COMMITMENT CYCLE

How to build confidence by taking
the leap before you're ready

Let me tell you the truth that most successful people won't say out loud: they were scared when they started. So was I.

But confidence doesn't come first.
Commitment does.

Every major transformation in my life, from building salons to starting global brands, started the same way: I said yes before I felt ready.

The Commitment Cycle goes like this:

1. Commit - You take the step.

2. Learn - You figure things out.

3. Grow - You get better.

4. Confidence - You realize, *I can actually do this.*

5. Repeat - Now that you have confidence, you're ready to commit to the next thing.

And around you go.

I used it when I walked away from corporate life and stepped into the beauty industry with zero experience.

I used it when I built Butterfly Loft, even though I knew nothing about construction. But I committed, learned, grew, and that gave me confidence to expand my empire with three more construction projects.

I put the commitment cycle into action again when I launched Pulp Riot and created Danger Jones.

I didn't start with the skills.
I started with the step.

How do you commit when you don't feel ready?
Here's what's worked for me:

1. Don't wait for clarity.

Clarity comes *after* commitment, not before it. You don't get to see the whole staircase. You only see one step. Take it anyway.

2. Expect fear. Move anyway.

If it scares you, good. That's a sign you're doing something that matters. Feel it, and then make the call, send the email, sign the lease, hit publish.

3. Make a punch list.

If something feels overwhelming, break it down into simpler tasks. Build momentum by doing one small thing that moves you forward. The cycle doesn't care how big the step is, only that you take it. Knock that item off the punch list, grow, and get the confidence you need to move on to the next task on the list. Repeat.

4. Borrow belief.

If you don't fully believe in yourself yet, borrow belief from someone who does. I had Alexis. I also had Ted. You might have a mentor, a friend, or even a book (like this one).

5. Don't look back.

Sometimes, once you commit, it's best to shut the door behind you. Many entrepreneurs call this "burning the bridge." Commit and watch the world react. Witness people appearing and circumstances arising that you could not have foreseen coming, that will help you on your journey up the spiral staircase.

Confidence isn't a prerequisite.
It's a byproduct.

If you want to design a life that matters, stop waiting to feel ready. Start moving. Let the Commitment Cycle do the rest. It's the engine behind the spiral staircase.

That's how I climbed.
And it's how you will too.

NOTE 3
DEFEAT GOLIATH – DO WHAT THEY CAN'T

**How to outmaneuver giants by building
with soul, speed, and substance**

I learned this early, back when I launched Level6 and realized something sobering: you can't outspend Goliath.

So how do you win?

You do what they can't. You find your edge, and you press it with everything you've got.

At first, I didn't know what that edge was.
But every step up the spiral showed me more:

- At our salon suites, we created the W Hotel for stylists: luxury, freedom, and design-forward spaces that the corporate guys couldn't imagine.

- At Butterfly Loft, we built deep, real relationships with our stylists, while the others handed out leases and treated artists like business transactions.

- At Butterfly Circus and Pulp Riot, we moved at the speed of sound while creating a movement on social media. We understood that it wasn't just what you posted, but how you connected.

- At Danger Jones, we made art. We built community. We created with quality, craftmanship, and taste, while others focused solely on increasing profits by cutting costs.

And at every turn, the corporate brands couldn't keep up. Not because we had more money. But because we were playing a different game.

So how do you beat the big guys by doing it differently?
Here's what's worked for me:

1. Move fast.

Goliath is slow. He needs approvals. Committees. Task Forces. Legal reviews. You need a group text, a plan, and the guts to launch it next week.

2. Prioritize soul over scale.

Legacy brands are built on spreadsheets. Your advantage is taste, vision, intention. Design everything with meaning: your packaging, your voice, your events. Make people feel something.

3. Give your community what they actually want.

Corporate brands talk about community. We actually build it. They create contracts. We create connection.

4. Be un-copyable.

If what you're doing can be replicated with money or a marketing team, it's not enough. Goliath shouldn't be able to do what you can do and look like they're doing it authentically. The secret is to do things that only you can pull off, with your story, your taste, and your community.

You don't need a bigger budget.
You need a better belief system.

Goliath can't build fast.
Can't build cool.
Can't build community.

But you can.

NOTE 4
SWING BIG WHEN YOU HAVE MOMENTUM

How to multiply your wins
by going bigger when the moment is hot

It can take a lot of work and ingenuity to get something to work. But once you get it to work, once something really has momentum, the best entrepreneurs don't just coast. They swing for the fences.

It's like poker. If you're holding a great hand, and you're given the chance to raise the stakes, the odds are stacked in your favor. Now is not the time to fold or even hold. It's time to go big.

I've done this over and over again. When we opened our first salon suites and they sold out instantly, I didn't wait. I built more. When Butterfly Circus sold out in seconds, I added a second show, then swung bigger when I put my own money at risk to book the big ballroom in New York. And when Pulp Riot got off to a hot start, we went big and invested heavily in a trade show booth that brought massive amounts of visibility to our brand.

When Danger Jones started to take off in the United States, we took a bigger swing when we pushed forward with global expansion.

So how do you swing for the fences?
Here's what's worked for me:

1. Watch for velocity.

Did something just sell out fast? Did the feed blow up? Did the buzz exceed your expectations? That's not luck. That's leverage. Use it.

2. Raise the stakes before the moment cools.

Momentum has a half-life. Don't overthink it. If something hits, act while the energy is still peaking.

3. Reinvest the win.

Take the attention and the buzz and pour it into the next play. This is how small sparks turn into wildfires.

4. Act like it's working, because it is.

Too many people win and still hesitate. Don't second guess your success. Trust the signals. Move with confidence.

5. Don't let perfection slow you down.

Speed matters when scaling. Others will see your momentum and try and replicate it. Stay out in front of them. If the second act isn't flawless, that's fine. Momentum matters more than polish. The energy of the moment will carry you.

Big brands wait for data.
Bold builders move on instinct.

If something's working, don't just celebrate it. Double down. Expand it. Elevate it. Swing for the fences.

That's how movements grow.
That's how legends are made.

BUILD CATHEDRALS, NOT ROCKET SHIPS

**How to build something that outlasts
trends, noise, and ego**

These days, everyone's building a brand.
Trying to launch the next big thing.
Trying to scale fast, go viral, and sell before it crashes.

That's the rocket ship model.
Build fast. Burn bright. Flip it if you can.

And I get it. I've done it. We sold Pulp Riot in 23 months.
The rocket worked. But I learned something that
changed everything: speed without soul doesn't satisfy.
Hype fades. But meaning endures.

So, this time, with Danger Jones, we're not building a
rocket. We're building a cathedral.

It takes longer. It requires deeper intention. But it's
worth it, because it's built to last.

We obsess over the details. We build community like
stained glass, one piece at a time. We make decisions
based on legacy, not short-term optics. It's not about
flash. It's about foundation.

So how do you build a cathedral instead of a rocket?
Here's what's helped me:

1. Start with what matters.

What do you want this thing to stand for twenty years from now? What kind of world should it shape? Start there.

2. Don't chase funding. Chase alignment.

Easy money is tempting. But cathedral builders raise belief before they raise capital.

3. Build for quality, not speed.

Don't rush the product. Don't chase what's trendy. Take the time to make something beautiful, useful, and timeless. Let it reflect your taste, not the market's noise.

4. Treat every detail like it matters.

Because it does. Your packaging. Your words. Your rituals. Every brick is part of the experience.

Rocket ships impress.
Cathedrals move people.

Build something people want to visit again.
Something that takes their breath away.
Something that lasts, not because it scaled fast,
but because it was worth building.

That's how you build a brand that becomes a legacy.
That's how you build something that changes culture.

That's how you build your cathedral.

NOTE 6
CREATE WHAT YOU CRAVE

How to turn dissatisfaction
into your creative blueprint

Sometimes, the next chapter of your life begins with a quiet thought: Why doesn't this exist yet?

That's how Danger Jones started. Not with a business plan. But with a craving.

After selling Pulp Riot, I took time off. Traveled. Rested. Reflected. And for a while, I felt free.

But then the ideas started creeping back in. The visions. The gaps I saw in the industry. The things I wished existed, not just in product, but in experience, in community, in energy.

And I realized: I wasn't done. I was just hungry again.

So, I started building the thing I craved.
Not what the market said it needed.
Not what would scale fastest.
But what my soul wanted to see in the world.

And that made all the difference.

So how do you turn your craving into something real?
Here's what's worked for me:

1. Notice your frustration.

What pisses you off? What feels fake, outdated, lifeless? There's gold in that discomfort. Let it point you toward what's missing.

2. Describe what you wish existed.

Not just the product, the feeling. How would it look? Smell? Sound? Make someone feel? Be weirdly specific. That's where the originality lives.

3. Assume you're not the only one.

If you crave it, others do too. They just might not know how to articulate it, yet. That's your job: give language and shape to the thing that's missing.

4. Build for yourself first.

Would you love it, even if it didn't "work"? If the answer is yes, you're on the right path. Authenticity doesn't need A/B testing.

5. Let your taste lead.

You don't need a focus group. You need to trust your eye, your gut, your conviction. Great things are often built by people with great taste.

Your craving isn't a flaw.
It's a compass.

It's pointing you toward what's possible.
Toward the thing you're here to make.
Toward the gap only you can fill.

So, stop waiting for someone else to do it.

If it doesn't exist, create it.
If it's not good enough, improve it.
If it's already great, remix it.

That's how new worlds begin.

NOTE 7
DESIGN A LIFE, NOT JUST A BRAND

**How to build a business that feeds your soul,
not just your bank account**

You can build a brand that looks amazing on the outside and still feel trapped inside it. I know, because I've lived it.

I've built the rocket ship.
Scaled it. Sold it.
Made the money. Took the year off.

But here's the truth I had to learn the hard way: success without alignment isn't freedom. It's a prettier kind of prison.

When I started over with Danger Jones, I wasn't just launching a brand. I was designing a life.

One built around:

- Creativity and adventure
- Relationships and beauty
- Meaningful work, done with people I love
- Freedom to travel, to build, to rest, to live

That's the deeper level most founders skip. They ask: "How do I scale this?" But they forget to ask: "Do I actually want the life this will create?"

So how do you build something that fuels your life?
Here's what's worked for me:

1. Define your ideal day, not just your ideal income.

What do you want your average Tuesday to look like? Start there. Then reverse-engineer a business that makes that possible.

2. Choose partners you actually want to spend time with.

You're going to be in the trenches with these people. If they don't inspire you, energize you, or challenge you... don't build with them.

3. Let your life become part of the brand.

We host events at our home. We travel with artists. We create from places we love. It's not just marketing, it's integration. The line between life and brand doesn't have to be a wall. It can be a bridge.

4. Check in often.

Are you still living the life you want? Or are you chasing a version of success you've outgrown? Realign as often as necessary. Evolution is the point.

Your brand is an expression.
Your life is the masterpiece.

Build something that lets you be fully alive.

Something that gives as much as it takes.

Something that creates freedom, not just income.

Because at the end of the day, it's not about how big your business gets. It's about how you feel while building it.

NOTE 8
GIVE THE MIC AWAY

How to elevate others instead
of hoarding the spotlight

Most people think the best way to lead is to be the loudest, smartest, or most visible person in the room. But here's what I've learned: If you want to build something bigger than yourself, you have to stop making it all about you.

That's how we did it at Butterfly Circus. Each artist had their moment. Each voice mattered.

At Pulp Riot and Danger Jones, we built entire communities by spotlighting stylists, not ourselves.

And that choice to celebrate others, to share influence, to pass the mic, is what created loyalty, momentum, and magic.

How do you give the mic away
and still grow your own brand?
Here's what's worked for me:

1. Spot talent early.

Look for people who are already showing up. They may not have a big following yet, but they've got the spark. Find them. Acknowledge them. Give them a chance to shine.

2. Create platforms for others to stand on.

At Danger Jones, we built Danger Fest, online spotlights, social features, certification programs. None of it is about us being the hero, it's about creating stages where they get to lead.

3. Share the wins.

Turn your feed into a gallery of others, not a shrine to yourself.

The goal isn't to be the genius in the room.
It's to make the room electric.

You'll know it's working when people feel ownership. When they show up not for a paycheck, but for a purpose. When they tell the world, "This is my brand too."

That's how movements are built.

Not by taking the mic.
But by giving it away.

NOTE 9
BUILD IN PUBLIC

How to turn your process into a marketing tool

Most people hide the mess. They wait until the launch is perfect. Until the brand is polished. Until the risk is over. But the truth is: people don't just want to see the result. They want to witness the becoming.

That's the gift of building in public.

I create it for the world to see. I shoot giant flares into the sky. I take people along for the process. It makes the people following along feel deeper about whatever I'm creating.

So how do you build in public without looking like a mess?
Here's what's worked for me:

1. Narrate the climb.

Tell people where you are. What you're trying to build. What's working. What's not. You don't need to have it all figured out, just be honest and intentional.

2. Show your work.

Share drafts. Sketches. Prototypes. Unboxings. Mistakes. Progress. Let people feel like they're part of it, not just the recipient of the finished product.

3. Talk like a human, not a brand.

Ditch the press release voice. Use your voice. Your face. Your truth. That's what people connect with.

4. Celebrate small wins in real time.

Sold out in 2 minutes? Show it. Got your first follower? Show it. People love watching momentum grow.

5. Let people grow with you.

The people who saw you build from nothing will always be your most loyal community. Don't just thank them, bring them along.

You don't need a perfect plan.
You need a public path.

Show them what you're making. Show them *why* it matters. Let them fall in love with the process, not just the product.

IT'S NOT SUPPOSED TO BE EASY

How to keep climbing when it's hard or uncertain

Let's end with this: If it feels hard, you're probably doing it right.

We live in a world that tries to sell ease. Quick wins. Passive income. Overnight success. But here's the truth they don't post: the climb is hard. It's supposed to be.

I've built things from scratch.
I've made painful decisions.
I've launched products that flopped.
I've had to fire people I cared about.
I've walked away from comfort to chase something that didn't yet exist.

And every time, I've faced the same feelings:

Fear.
Doubt.
Loneliness.
Exhaustion.
The temptation to go back to something easier.

But I kept going.

Why?

Because I knew this: Struggle isn't a signal to stop. It's proof you're building something real.

So how do you keep going when it gets hard?
Here's what's helped me:

1. Expect resistance.

It's not personal. It's part of the process. If you're breaking new ground, you're going to hit rocks. Keep digging.

2. Normalize the lows.

You will feel lost sometimes. You will question everything. That doesn't mean you're broken. It means you're becoming.

3. Stay close to the mission.

When the money's not flowing and the praise isn't coming... the mission has to be enough. Remind yourself why you started. Read your own manifesto. Then get back to work.

4. Talk to people who get it.

Find others who are building hard things. Share the real story. You don't need more advice. You need more connection.

5. Zoom out.

Hard day? Step back. Look at how far you've come. One step doesn't define the climb. One bad week doesn't rewrite your trajectory.

The spiral is steep.
But that's what makes it worth climbing.

You're not doing it wrong because it's hard. You're doing it right, and you're still in motion. So don't stop now.

Take a breath.
Feel your feet.
And take the next step.

Because it's not about getting there.
It's about becoming who you were meant to be.

Books spread the same way movements do, through the people who believe in them. If this one spoke to you, a short review on Amazon would mean a lot. That's how indie creators like me keep building momentum.

I'm still climbing.

Want to follow along?

@davidthurstonofficial on social media.

www.thurstonproductions.com

ACKNOWLEDGEMENTS

This book, like every beautiful thing I've ever been a part of, was never built alone. It's the result of countless people moving in rhythm, believing, building, creating, and climbing together.

To **Alexis**, my partner in life and creation. Thank you for dreaming with me, for your relentless pursuit of excellence, and for standing shoulder to shoulder with me through every twist of the staircase. Everything I build is better because you're in it.

To **Stevie**, who carries the flame when I'm chasing the next horizon. Thank you for your leadership, loyalty, and friendship. You've turned visions into movements.

To **Kasey and Doug** for being two people I can always count on. I'll always be grateful for the sacrifices you've made over the years for our community and the success of our mission.

To our **team at Danger Jones**. You've helped transform an idea into a living, breathing brand that has impacted artists around the globe. Thank you for your belief, your grind, and your heart. I love creating with you.

To the **artists** who have colored this journey with your creativity and love. To everyone who has shared a stage, an airplane, a laugh, or a moment of inspiration with me. I see you, I feel you, and I thank you. I appreciate the trust. I'm building this for us.

To our **distribution partners** across forty-something countries. Thank you for spreading this message around the world and proving that artistry transcends borders.

To the **investors and believers** who've backed us not just with capital but with conviction. You've given us the resources to dream bigger.

To **my parents** for being the greatest.

To **Bowie and Finley** for making sacrifices along the way that have allowed us to climb. Love you both.

The Spiral Staircase was built by the Power of Many.

LISTEN FREE

Scan the QR code or visit
http://www.thurstonproductions.com/audio-spiral-lfg
to stream or download a free audio recording of this book,
narrated by the author.